An American National Standard

IEEE Standards for Local Area Networks:

Supplements to Carrier Sense Multiple Access with Collision Detection (CSMA/CD) Access Method and Physical Layer Specifications

Published by
The Institute of Electrical and Electronics Engineers, Inc

ANSI/IEEE
Std 802.3b, c, d, and e
1989 Edition
(IEEE Supplements to ISO 8802-3 : 1989
[ANSI/IEEE Std 802.3-1988])

An American National Standard

IEEE Standards for Local Area Networks:

Supplements to Carrier Sense Multiple Access with Collision Detection (CSMA/CD) Access Method and Physical Layer Specifications

---

Sections 9.1-9.8:
ANSI/IEEE Std 802.3c-1985*, Repeater Unit for 10 Mb/s Baseband Networks

Section 9.9:
ANSI/IEEE Std 802.3d-1987, Medium Attachment Unit and Baseband Medium Specification for a Vendor Independent Fiber Optic Inter Repeater Link

Section 11:
ANSI/IEEE Std 802.3b-1985*, Broadband Medium Attachment Unit and Broadband Medium Specifications, Type 10BROAD36

Section 12:
ANSI/IEEE Std 802.3e-1987*, Physical Signaling, Medium Attachment, and Baseband Medium Specifications, Type 1BASE5

Sponsor

Technical Committee on Computer Communications of the IEEE Computer Society

[*The years in these designations have been changed from those printed in the 1988 Edition to reflect the IEEE Standards Board approval date rather than the year of publication.]

First Printing
July 1989

ISBN 1-55937-013-0

Library of Congress Catalog Number 89-083672

The Institute of Electrical and Electronics Engineers, Inc
345 East 47th Street, New York, NY 10017 USA

Foreword

(This Foreword is not a part of ANSI/IEEE Std 802.3b, c, d, and e, 1989 Edition, Supplements to Carrier Sense Multiple Access with Collision Detection (CSMA/CD) Access Method and Physical Layer Specifications.)

Part I

These supplements to ANSI/IEEE Std 802.3 are part of a family of standards for Local Area Networks (LANs). The relationship between this standard and other members of the family is shown below. (The numbers in the figure refer to IEEE standard numbers.)

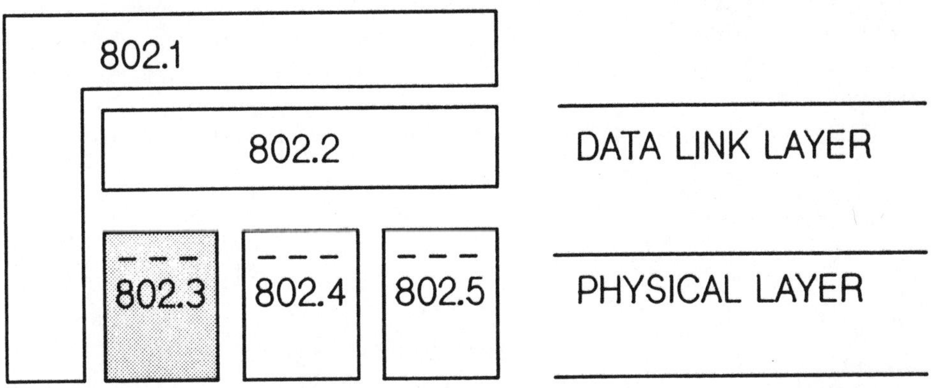

This family of standards deals with the Physical and Data Link Layers as defined by the ISO Open System Interconnection Reference Model. The access standards define three types of medium access technologies and associated physical media, each appropriate for particular applications or system objectives. The standards defining these technologies are:

(1) ISO 8802-3 : 1989 [ANSI/IEEE Std 802.3-1988], a bus utilizing CSMA/CD as the access method,

(2) ANSI/IEEE Std 802.4-1985 [pending ISO 8802-4], a bus utilizing token passing as the access method,

(3) ANSI/IEEE Std 802.5-1985 [pending ISO 8802-5], a ring utilizing token passing as the access method.

ANSI/IEEE Std 802.2-1985 [pending ISO 8802-2], the Logical Link Control standard, is used in conjunction with the medium access standards.

IEEE P802.1 describes the relationship among these standards and their relationship to the ISO Open Systems Interconnection Reference Model in more detail. This companion document also will contain networking management standards and information on internetworking. The reader of this standard is urged to become familiar with the complete family of standards.

The local area network access mechanism specified by this standard may include patented matter. The IEEE Standards Office calls attention to the fact that it is claimed that the process of the local area network access mechanism described throughout this standard is the subject of United States patent numbers 4 063 220 and 4 099 024 and corresponding patents of foreign countries owned by the Xerox Corporation. Although these patents appear to cover the access mechanism subject in this standard, the IEEE takes no position with respect to patent validity. The Xerox Corporation has assured the IEEE that it is willing to grant a license under these patents on reasonable and nondiscriminatory terms and conditions to anyone wishing to obtain such a license. The Xerox Corporation's undertakings in this respect are on file with the IEEE Standards Office and the license details may be obtained from the Office of General Counsel of Xerox Corporation, whose address is Post Office Box 1600, Stamford, CT 06904, USA.

This standard contains state-of-the-art material. The area covered by this standard is undergoing evolution. Revisions are anticipated to this standard within the next few years to clarify existing material, to correct possible errors, and to incorporate new related material.

Readers wishing to know the state of revisions should contact:

Secretary
IEEE Standards Board
345 East 47th Street
New York, NY 10017
USA

Part II

Historical Overview

It has long been the intent of the IEEE 802.3 Working Group to add new physical media sections as the need for such additions was justified. There were, in fact, placeholders for Section 10, Baseband Medium Specifications and Section 11, Broadband Medium Specifications in the original ANSI/IEEE Std 802.3-1985. It was further recognized at the time the initial IEEE 802.3 Standard was developed that Section 9, Repeater Unit, was not totally complete and would have to be revised at some future time.

Within the past few years it has become feasible to consider the use of already installed twisted pair wiring, commonly used in the telephone industry, as a basic medium for transmission of local area network digital data. A specification has been developed to support this type of medium.

This standard contains four basic supplements to the IEEE 802.3 Standard:

(1) Sections 9.1 through 9.8, Repeater Unit for 10 Mb/s Baseband Networks, Supplement c

(2) Section 9.9, Medium Attachment Unit and Baseband Medium Specification for a Vendor Independent Fiber Optic Inter Repeater Link, Supplement d

(3) Section 11, Broadband Medium Attachment Unit and Broadband Medium Specifications, Type 10BROAD36, Supplement b

(4) Section 12, Physical Signaling, Medium Attachment, and Baseband Medium Specifications, Type 1BASE5, Supplement e

Relationships to IEEE Standard 802.3, Sections 1-7

This Supplement standard is intended to be a companion document to ISO 8802-3 : 1989 [ANSI/IEEE Std 802.3-1988], with which the reader should be thoroughly familiar.

It is intended that ISO 8802-3 Sections 1-7 form the base specification for all of these supplements. Each specification with a "TYPE" designation is a specification for an alternate medium to be used in the CSMA/CD Access Method. Therefore, one, and only one, of these medium types may be used in any given implementation. It should be noted, of course, that it is possible to interconnect different implementations in a hierarchical fashion to satisfy certain application requirements (eg, Type 10BASE2 LANs interconnected to a Type 10BASE5 backbone LAN, etc).

The reader should understand that the use of Type 10BASE2 medium requires utilization of Sections 1-7, 9, 10, and ignores use of Section 8, 11, and 12. Similarly, the use of Type 10BROAD36 medium requires use of Sections 1-7 and Section 11 and ignores Sections 8, 9, 10, and 12. The use of twisted pair medium, Type 1BASE5, requires consideration of Sections 1-6 and Section 12, ignoring Sections 7-11.

The notation used throughout the IEEE 802.3 Standard family for identifying different physical layer capabilities is included here for convenient reference and is a duplication of Section 1.2.3 of the ISO standard.

> **1.2.3. Physical Layer and Media Notation.** Users of this standard need to reference which particular implementation is being used or identified. Therefore, a means of identifying each implementation is given by a simple, three-field, type notation that is explicitly stated at the beginning of each relevant section. In general, the Physical Layer type is specified by these fields.
>
> <data rate in Mb/s> <medium type> <maximum segment length (× 100m)>
>
> For example, the standard contains a 10Mb/s baseband specification identified as: "TYPE 10BASE5", meaning a 10Mb/s baseband medium whose maximum segment length is 500 m. Each successive Physical Layer specification will state is own unique TYPE identifier along similar lines.

At the time IEEE Standard 802.3 was first published, a basic decision was made to include the definition of a Repeater Unit, even though not all aspects of the Repeater Unit itself were completely defined. The decision to do this was made on the basis that a comprehensive CSMA/CD system would require a Repeater Unit and a complete list of system parameters was essential. In particular, the system parameters having to do with various delays throughout the system from DTE to DTE and system jitter budgets were essential considerations for complete system design. In summary, the overall system budgets were included in the original specification for the Repeater Unit; however, the means to achieve them within the Repeater Unit were not completely specified. The specifications presented in the 1985 publication were necessary, but not sufficient for a complete Repeater Unit implementation. It is believed the Repeater Unit specifications contained in this edition of the IEEE 802.3 Standard are both necessary and sufficient for a complete Repeater Unit implementation. It is to be pointed out that one embodiment of repeater functionality can be implemented using optical fiber medium. This capability is known as a Fiber Optic Inter Repeater Link, and its specifications and performance are very closely related to those of the

Repeater Unit itself. Section 9.9 of the Repeater Unit contains such an optical inter repeater link.

The reader should note that several isolated paragraphs throughout Sections 1–7 make reference to the initial Type 10BASE5 implementation as this was in fact the subject of the first 802.3 Standard. The reader is cautioned to read these sections "liberally" to permit interpretation and use with media other than Type 10BASE5. In most instances, there are no technical specifications involved, rather, comments and descriptions relating to the general application and scope of the CSMA/CD Access Method. The one section that may contain parameters and values unique to a particular implementation are contained in Section 4.2, Allowable Implementations. The reader should pay particular attention to any reference to these values when implementing a specific medium. Those subsections that refer to media dependent statements in a general way are: 1.1.1 Basic Concepts, and 1.2.3 Physical Layer and Media Notation.

Relationship to ISO 8802-3

ANSI/IEEE Std 802.3-1985 has been replaced by ISO 8802 :, an international standard. Publication ISO 8802-3 : 1988 [ANSI/IEEE Std 802.3-1988] is the revision of ANSI/IEEE 802.3-1985 with editorial and clarification changes and without substantive technical changes. The ISO ANSI/IEEE Standard Carrier Sense Multiple Access with Collision Detection specifies the Type 10BASE5 medium as contained in ANSI/IEEE Std 802.3-1985, along with the Type 10BASE2 Specification defined in Section 10. The first printing of this joint ISO/ANSI/IEEE Standard supercedes the original 1985 edition.

The Supplements contained in this IEEE publication have also been submitted to ISO for consideration as addenda to ISO 8802-3. They are not yet, however, fully approved as ISO standards and therefore, are being printed only as IEEE standards in a separate publication on an interim basis. It is the intention, when these supplements are fully approved by ISO as addenda to 8802-3, that they will be incorporated in a single complete edition of joint ISO/ANSI/IEEE CSMA/CD Media Access Specifications.

IEEE 802.3 Related Specifications Under Consideration

It is anticipated that a few additional media will eventually be added to the basic ISO 8802-3 [IEEE 802.3] specification along with clarification from the normal revision cycle based on practical use and application of the CSMA/CD concepts.

Errata

[These changes and additions are considered part of ANSI/IEEE Std 802.3-1989 Edition Supplements.]

The addition of these supplements has necessitated several minor changes to the base CSMA/CD standard to accommodate the new media and repeater specifications. These additions or revisions are identified in the following material and make the text of the published ISO 8802-3 standard consistent with these supplements.

1. Introduction

1.1.1 Basic Concepts

[change last sentence to read:]

This supplementary edition of the standard provides the necessary specifications for additional 10Mb/s baseband and broadband specifications, 1Mb/s baseband specification, and revised Repeater Unit specification.

1.1.2.2

[add to last paragraph:]

The AUI may be optional or not specified for some implementations of this standard that are expected to be connected directly to the medium and so do not use a separate MAU or its interconnecting AUI cable. The PLS and PMA are then part of a single unit, and no explicit AUI specification is required.

1.2.1 State Diagram Conventions

[add to section:]

Some of the devices described in this standard (repeaters and hubs) are allowed to have two or more ports. State diagrams capable of describing the operation of devices with an unspecified number of ports, required qualifier notation that allows testing for conditions at multiple ports. The notation used is a term that includes a description in parentheses of which ports must meet the term for the qualifier to be satisfied (eg, ANY and ALL). It is also necessary to provide for term-assignment statements that assign a name to a port that satisfies a qualifier. The following convention is used to describe a term-assignment statement that is associated with a transition:

(1) The character ":" (colon) is a delimiter used to denote that a term assignment statement follows.

(2) The character "⇐" (left arrow) denotes assignment of the value following the arrow to the term preceding the arrow.

The state diagrams contain the authoritative statement of the functions they depict; when apparent conflicts between descriptive text and state diagrams arise, the state diagrams are to take precedence. This does not override, however, any explicit description in the text that has no parallel in the state diagrams.

The models presented by state diagrams are intended as the primary specifications of the functions to be provided. It is important to distinguish, however, between a model and a real implementation. The models are optimized for simplicity and clarity of presentation, while any realistic implementation may place heavier emphasis on efficiency and suitability to a particular implementation technology. It is the functional behavior of any unit that must match the standard, not its internal structure. The internal details of the model are useful only to the extent that they specify the external behavior clearly and precisely.

1.3 References

[replace section:]

[1] CISPR Publication 22 (1985), Limits and Methods of Measurement of Radio Interference Characteristics of Information Technology Equipment.[1]

[2] IEC Publication 96-1 (1971) (3rd Edition), Radio Frequency Cable, Part 1: General Requirements and Measuring Methods.[2]

[3] IEC Publication 96-1A (1976), 1st Supplement, Radio Frequency Cable, Part 1: Appendix Section 5.4, Terminated Triaxial Test Method for Transfer Impedance up to 100 MHz.

[4] IEC Publication 169-8 and -16, Radio Frequency Coaxial Connections with Screw Coupling, 50 Ω (Type BNC and Type N).

[5] IEC Publication 380 (1985) (3rd Edition), Safety of Electrically Energized Office Machines.

[6] IEC Publication 435 (1983) (2nd Edition), Safety of Data Processing Equipment.

[7] IEC Publication 807-2 (1985) (1st Edition), Detail Specification for a Range of Connectors with Round Contacts—Fixed Solder Contact Types.

[8] IEC Publication 950 (1986), Safety of Information Technology Equipment Including Electrical Business Equipment.

[9] ISO 2382/09, The Information Processing Vocabulary, IPV, Section 09: Data Communication.[3]

---

[1] CISPR documents are available in the US from the Sales Department, American National Standards Institute, 1430 Broadway, New York, NY 10018, USA. These documents are also available from International Electrotechnical Commission, 3 rue de Varembé, Case Postale 131, CH-1211, Genève 20, Switzerland/Suisse.

[2] IEC documents are available in the US from the Sales Department, American National Standards Institute, 1430 Broadway, New York, NY 10018, USA. IEC documents are also available from International Electrotechnical Commission, 3 rue de Varembé, Case Postale 131, CH-1211, Genève 20, Switzerland/Suisse.

[3] ISO documents are available in the US from the Sales Department, American National Standards Institute, 1430 Broadway, New York, NY 10018, USA. ISO documents are also available from the ISO office, 1 rue de Varembé, Case Postale 56, CH-1211, Genève 20, Switzerland/Suisse.

[10] ISO 7498, Information Processing Systems — Open Systems Interconnection — Basic Reference Model, November 15, 1984.

[11] IEC Publication 60, High-Voltage Test Methods.

[12] IEC Publication 793-1, Optical Fibers.

[13] IEC Publication 874-2, Connectors for Optical Fibers and Cables, Part 2 — Sectional Specifications for Fiber Optic Connector Type F-SMA.

[14] IEC Document 76 (Central Office) 6, Radiation Safety of Laser Products and Equipment-Classification, Requirements, and User's Guide.

[15] IEC Publication 68, Basic Environmental Testing Procedures.

[16] ISO/DIS 8877, Interface Connector and Contact Assignments for ISDN Basic Access Interface Located at Reference Points S and T.

1.4 Definitions

The definitions used in this standard are consistent with ISO 2382/09, the Information Processing Vocabulary, IPV, Part 09, Data Communication. A more specific IPV Part 25 pertaining to LAN systems is in development.

4. Media Access Control

4.4.2.1 Parameterized Values

[add to section:]
See also DTE Deference Delay in 12.9.2.

4.4.2.2 Parameterized Values

[add to section:]

The following parameter values shall be used for 1BASE5 implementations:

Parameter	Value
slotTime	512 bit-times
interFrameGap	96 μs
attemptLimit	16
backoffLimit	10
jamSize	32 bits
maxFrameSize	1518 octets
minFrameSize	512 bits (64 octets)
addressSize	48 bits

See also DTE Deference Delay in 12.9.2.

WARNING: Any deviation from the above specified values may affect proper operation of the network.

4.4.2.3 Parameterized Values. Other implementations under consideration.

7. Physical Signaling (PLS) and Attachment Unit Interface (AUI) Specifications

7.2.4 PLS Functions

[add to first paragraph]

These functions are depicted in the state diagrams shown in Figs 7-3 through 7-8, using notation described in 1.2.1.

The following individuals were voting members of the IEEE 802.3 Working Group for one or more of the supplements (b, c, d, and e) to ANSI/IEEE Std 802.3-1988:

Don Loughry, *Chairman*
Gary Robinson, *Vice Chairman*

Menachem Abraham
Keith Albright
Keith Amundsen
Jean-Pierre Astorg
R. V. Balakrishnan
Ian Barker
William Belknap
Richard Bennett
Charles Brill
Juan Bulnes
Robert Campbell
Luigi Canavese
Albert Claessen
Stephen Cooper
Michael Coden
Ronald Crane
Bill Cronin
John Davidson
Peter Dawe
Peter Desaulniers
Mark Devon
Raymond Duley
Paul Eastman
Jeff Ebeling
Phil Edholm
Gregory Ennis
Gianfranco Enrico
Judy Estrin
Alan Flatman
Richard Fransen
Ingrid Fromm
Robert Galin
Sharad Gandhi
Mark Gerhold
Adi Golbert
Rich Graham
Richard Gumpertz
Hacene Hariti
Guy Harkins
Lloyd Hasley
Haw Ming Haung
Charles Hoffner
Gregory Hopkins
Fred Huang
Michael Hughes
Stephen Janshego
Donald Johnson
Mike Johnson
Kwi-Yung Jung
Matt Kaltenbach
Paul Kellam
Joe Kennedy
Scott Kesler
Hiroshi Kobayashi
Hidetsune Kurokawa
Lee LaBarre
Ed Lare
Michael Lee
Wayne Lindquist
William Livingston
Terry Lockyer
Hugh Logan
Leland Long
James Lucas
Andy Luque
Daniel Maltbie
Luciano Marchitto
Joseph Mazor
Steven Moustakas
Narayan Murthy
Wendell Nakamine
Lloyd Oliver
Aidan Paul
Roy Pierce
Bill Poston
David Potter
Eric Rawson
Eugene Reilly
Joseph Rickert
Anthony Rizzolo
Timothy Rock
David Roos
Robert Rosenthal
Joseph St. Amand
Ed Sakaguchi
Walter Schreuer
Semir Sirazi
David Smith
Stephen Soto
Gary Spencer
Robert Summers
Pat Thaler
Mark Taylor
Peter Tarrant
Pat Thaler
Geoff Thompson
Nathan Tobol
Carlos Tomaszewski
Wendell Turner
Jayshree Ullal
Marc Warshaw
David White
Lawrence White
Bruce Williams
Rich Williams
Joseph Wiencko
Ronald Yara
Mo Zonoun

The following individuals were observers of the IEEE 802.3 Working Group and contributed to one or more of the supplements to ANSI/IEEE Std 802.3-1988:

Rien Baan
Brad Blau
Mark Bohrer
Allen Cherin
Jacques Christ
Robert Conte
John DeCramer
Gennaro DiGiuseppe
Shinji Emori
David Fischer
Jiro Kashio
Larry Lipke
Luciano Marchitto
Jim Montrose
Gaurang Shah
Michael Yuen
Eric Zahnd

Appreciation is expressed to dozens of people who attended 802.3 Plenary or Task Force meetings and also contributed to the elaboration of these supplemental standards.

ANSI/IEEE
Std 802.3c-1985
Std 802.3d-1987
(Supplements to ANSI/IEEE Std 802.3-1988)

An American National Standard

Repeater Unit for 10 Mb/s Baseband Networks (Section 9)

Sponsor
IEEE Computer Society

[802.3c-1986, Sections 9.1-9.8]

Approved December 12, 1985
IEEE Standards Board

Approved June 4, 1986
American National Standards Institute

[802.3d-1987, Section 9.9]

Approved December 10, 1987
IEEE Standards Board

Approved February 9, 1989
American National Standards Institute

When the IEEE 802.3 Working Group approved this standard (802.3c, Sections 9.1-9.8) in July 1985, it had the following membership:

Don Loughry, *Chairman*
Geoff Thompson, *Chairman, Repeater Task Force*

Menachem Abraham
Keith Albright
R. V. Balakrishnan
William Belknap
Richard Bennett
Charles Brill
Juan Bulnes
Stephen Cooper
Paul Eastman
Phil Edholm
Gregory Ennis
Alan Flatman
Richard Fransen
Ingrid Fromm
Robert Galin
Sharad Gandhi
Rich Graham
Richard Gumpertz
Hacene Hariti
Guy Harkins
Fred Huang
Stephen Janshego
Donald Johnson
Kwi-Yung Jung
Paul Kellam
Joe Kennedy
Hiroshi Kobayashi
Lee LaBarre
Tony Lauck
John Laynor
William Livingston
Terry Lockyer
James Lucas
Andy Luque
Daniel Maltbie
Steven Moustakas
Lloyd Oliver
Aidan Paul
David Potter
Eric Rawson
Joseph Rickert
Gary Robinson
Timothy Rock
David Roos
Robert Rosenthal
Joseph St. Amand
Walter Schreuer
Semir Sirazi
David Smith
Stephen Soto
Robert Summers
Pat Thaler
Wendell Turner
Marc Warshaw
Ronald Yara

The following persons were on the balloting committee that approved this document (802.3c) for submission to the IEEE Standards Board:

Marshall Abrams
John Adams
William B. Adams
S. R. Ahuja
P. D. Amer
Kit Athul
William Ayen
Yong-Myung Baeg
Wesley A. Ballenger, Jr
Edwardo W. Bergamini
H. F. Boley
Paul W. Campbell, Jr
George S. Carson
Po Chen
L. Y. Cheung
Kilnam Chon
T. Ricky Chow
W. F. Chow
David Cohen
Allen F. Conrad
Robert S. Crowder
Michel Diaz
Philip H. Enslow, Jr
Judith Estrin
John W. Fendrich
Harvey A. Freeman
R. J. Gagliano
Patrick Gonia
Ambuj Goyal
Michael D. Graebner
Maris Graube
Nobushiro Hamada
Joseph L. Hammond
S. M. Harris
J. Scott Haugdahl
C. W. Hobbs
Jim P. Hong
Paul L. Hutton
Richard Iliff
George D. Jelatis
E. D. Jensen
Guy Juanole
Karl H. Kellermayr
Mladen Kozunovic
Samuel Kho
David Kollm
Sastri L. Kota
Hirayr M. Kudyan
Takahiko Kuki
Lee LaBarre
Wai-Sum Lai
Lanse M. Leach
Stephen E. Levin
F. C. Lim
William Livingston
Don C. Loughry
Joseph F. P. Luhukay
Meli Marco
Marco Marsan
Joseph Massi

Darrell B. McIndoe
Patrick S. McIntosh
David S. Millman
Aditya N. Mishra
David E. Morgan
Mike Morganti
Kinji Mori
D. J. Morris
H. T. Mouftah
Dale A. Murray
Ruth Nelson
J. Duane Northcutt
Charles Oestereicher
Young Oh
George Parowski
Thomas L. Phinney
David Potter
John Potvcek
Gary S. Robinson
Marya Repko
Robert Rosenthal
Gian Paolo Rossi
David J. Rypka
S. I. Samoylenko
Norman F. Schneidewind
Oscar Sepulveda
Omri Serlin
D. Sheppard
R. M. Simmons
Dr. L. Sintonen
David W. Sloyer
Stephen Soto
Fred Strauss
Bart W. Stuck
Tatsuya Suda
Efstathios D. Sykas
Daniel T. W. Sze
Ahmed N. Tantaui
Mario Tokoro
H. C. Torng
Donald F. Towsley
Wei-Tek Tsai
M. Tsuchiya
Richard Tung
Stanko Turk
L. David Umbaugh
James Vorhies
Pearl S. C. Wang
Don Weir
Alan J. Weissberger
William J. Wenker
Earl J. Whitaker
Michael Willett
Tsong-Ho Wu
Oren Yuen

When the IEEE Standards Board approved this standard on December 12, 1985, it had the following membership:

John E. May, *Chairman* **John P. Riganati,** *Vice Chairman*

Sava I. Sherr, *Secretary*

James H. Beall
Fletcher J. Buckley
Rene Castenschiold
Edward Chelotti
Edward J. Cohen
Paul G. Cummings
Donald C. Fleckenstein
Jay Forster
Daniel L. Goldberg
Kenneth D. Hendrix
Irvin N. Howell
Jack Kinn
Joseph L. Koepfinger*
Irving Kolodny
R. F. Lawrence
Lawrence V. McCall
Donald T. Michael*
Frank L. Rose
Clifford O. Swanson
J. Richard Weger
W. B. Wilkens
Charles J. Wylie

*Member emeritus

When the IEEE 802.3 Working Group approved this standard (802.3d, Section 9.9), it had the following membership:

Steven Moustakas, *Chairman, Task Force*

Menachem Abraham
Keith Albright
Keith Amundsen
Jean-Pierre Astorg
R. V. Balakrishnan
Richard Bennett
Charles Brill
Juan Bulnes
Robert Campbell
Luigi Canavese
Albert Claessen
Peter Dawe
Peter Desaulniers
Raymond Duley
Jeff Ebeling
Gianfranco Enrico
Alan Flatman
Richard Fransen
Ingrid Fromm
Robert Galin
Mark Gerhold
Adi Golbert
Rich Graham
Rich Gumpertz
Hacene Hariti
Lloyd Hasley
Hawming Haung
Charles Hoffner
Michael Hughes
Donald Johnson
Mize Johnson
Kwi-Yung Jung
Matt Kaltenbach
Paul Kellam
Scott Kesler
Hiroshi Kobayashi
Hidetsune Kurokawa
Lee LaBarre
Ed Lare
Wayne Lindquist
Terry Lockyer
Don Loughry
James Lucas
Andy Luque
Lloyd Oliver
Aidan Paul
Roy Pierce
Eric Rawson
Joseph Rickert
Gary Robinson
Timothy Rock
David Roos
Walter Schruer
Semir Sirazi
David Smith
Robert Summers
Pat Thaler
Geoff Thompson
Nathan Tobol
Carlos Tomaszewski
Wendell Turner
Joseph Wiencko
Bruce Williams

OBSERVERS

Allen Cherin
John Decramer
Paul Eastman
Shinji Emori
Jiro Kashio
Michael Lee
Marchitto Luciano
Jim Montrose
Peter Tarrant

The IEC TC83 Committee on Information Technology Equipment also provided very helpful input to the development of the FOIRL Standard.

When the IEEE Standards Board approved this standard on December 10, 1987, it had the following membership:

Donald C. Fleckenstein, *Chairman* **Marco W. Migliaro,** *Vice Chairman*
Andrew G. Salem, *Secretary*

James H. Beall
Dennis Bodson
Marshall L. Cain
James M. Daly
Stephen R. Dillon
Eugene P. Fogarty
Jay Forster
Kenneth D. Hendrix
Irvin N. Howell
Leslie R. Kerr
Jack Kinn
Irving Kolodny
Joseph L. Koepfinger*
Edward Lohse
John May
Lawrence V. McCall
L. Bruce McClung
Donald T. Michael*
L. John Rankine
John P. Riganati
Gary S. Robinson
Frank L. Rose
Robert E. Rountree
William R. Tackaberry
William B. Wilkens
Helen M. Wood

* Member emeritus

The following persons were on the balloting committee that approved this document (802.3d) for submission to the IEEE Standards Board:

William B. Adams
S. R. Ahuja
Kit Athul
William Ayen
Eduardo W. Bergamini
Paul W. Campbell, Jr
George S. Carson
Po Chen
L. Y. Cheung
Kilnam Chon
W. F. Chow
Michael Coden
A. F. Conrad
Robert S. Crowder
Michel Diaz
N. I. Dimopoulos
M. G. Duncan
Philip H. Enslow, Jr
Judith Estrin
John W. Fendrich
Harvey A. Freeman
Patrick S. Gonia
R. L. Gordon
A. Goyal
M. D. Graebner
Maris Graube
Joseph L. Hammond
Stephen Harris
J. Scott Haugdahl
C. W. Hobbs
Paul Hutton
Richard Iliff
E. D. Jenson
Guy Juanole
Karl H. Kellermayr
M. Kezunovic
Samuel Kno
S. E. Kille
David Kollm
Takahiko Kuki
Lee LaBarre
Wai-Sum Lai
Lanse M. Leach
Edward Y. Lee
R. C. Lightburn
F. C. Lim
William D. Livingston
Don C. Loughry
Joseph F. P. Luhukay
Wo-Shun Luk
Marco Ajmone Marsan
Joseph Massi
Marco Meli
Darrel B. McIndoe
P. S. McIntosh
David S. Millman
Aditya N. Mishra
David E. Morgan
Mike Morganti
Kanji Mori
David Morris
H. H. T. Mouftah
Dale N. Murray
R. R. Nelson
J. D. Northcut
Charles Oestereicher
Young Oh
George Parowski
Thomas L. Phinney
J.M. Potucek
Marya Repko
Gary S. Robinson
Robert Rosenthal
Gian Paolo Rossi
David J. Rypka
S. I. Samaylenko
Norman F. Schneidewind
Omri Serlin
D. Sheppard
Ron Simmons
J. B. Sinclair
L. Sintonen
Tom Stack
Carel M. Stillebroer
Fred Strauss
Tatsuya Suda
P. Sugar
Efstathios D. Sykas
Daniel T. W. Sze
Ahmed N. Tantawi
H. C. Torng
D. F. Towsley
Wei-Tek Tsai
Stanko Turk
L. David Umbaugh
J. T. Vorhies
Pearl S. C. Wang
Don Weir
Alan J. Weissburger
W. J. Wenker
Earl J. Whitaker
Bryan Whittle
Michael Willett
David C. Wood
Tsong-Hu Wu
Oren Yuen

Contents

FIGURES PAGE

9. Repeater Unit for 10 Mb/s Baseband Networks

9.1 Overview. This section specifies a repeater for use with type 10BASE5 and 10BASE2 networks. A repeater for any other ISO 8802-3 network type is beyond the scope of this section.

A repeater set connects segments of network medium together thus allowing larger topologies and a larger MAU base than are allowed by rules governing individual setments (that is for 10BASE5, 500 m and 100 stations, for 10BASE2, 185 m and 30 stations).

Repeater sets are used to extend the network length and topology beyond what could be achieved by a single coaxial segment as defined in 8.6 or 10.7. Segments may be connected directly by a repeater set (Fig 9-1) or by pairs of repeater units which are, in turn connected by inter repeater links. Allowable topologies shall contain only one operative signal path between any two points on the network. A maximum of four repeater sets may be in the signal path between any two stations on the network (this assumes two Inter Repeater Links).

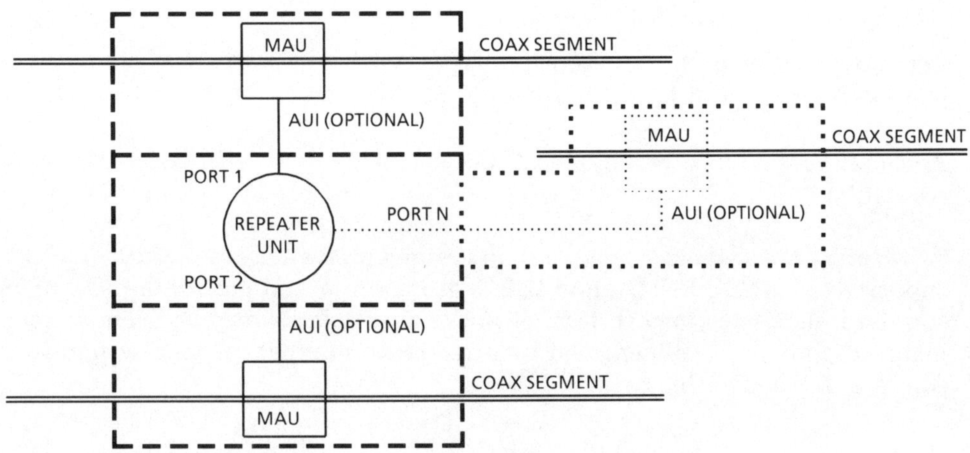

Fig 9-1
Repeater Set, Coax-to-Coax Configuration

Note: The AUI is not necessarily exposed when the MAU is, optionally, part of the physical repeater.

If the repeater set uses MAUs connected via AUIs to a repeater unit, the external MAUs shall be basic MAUs with the exception of the *signal_quality_error* test function. A manufacturer may optionally integrate one or all MAUs into a single package with the repeater unit (internal MAUs). In all cases the MAU portion of the repeater set must be counted toward the maximum number of MAUs on each segment as specified in 8.6 and 10.7. A repeater set is not a station and does not count toward the overall limit of 1024 stations on a network.

A repeater set can receive and decode data from any segment under worst case noise, timing, and signal amplitude conditions. It retransmits the data to all other segments attached to it with timing and amplitude restored. The retransmission of data occurs simultaneously with reception. If a collision occurs, the repeater set propagates the collision event throughout the network by transmitting a Jam signal.

9.2 Definitions

Data Frame. Consists of the Destination Address, Source Address, Length Field, LLC Data, Pad, and Frame Check Sequence.

IRL (Inter Repeater Link). A mechanism for interconnecting two and only two repeater units.

Packet. Consists of a Data Frame as defined previously, preceded by the Preamble and the Start Frame Delimiter.

Port. A setment or IRL interface of a repeater unit.

Repeater Unit. The portion of a repeater set that is inboard of its PMA/PLS interfaces.

Repeater Set. A repeater unit plus its associated MAUs and, if present, AU Interfaces (AUIs).

9.3 References. Local and national standards references such as those supported by ANSI, ECMA, and IEEE, are not a formal part of the ISO 8802-3 standard. Reference to such local or national standards may be useful resource material and they are identified by a reference number [n] and located in the Annex at the end of this book.

9.4 Compatibility Interface. The repeater shall attach to its network segments by any of the means specified below.

9.4.1 AUI Compatibility. The repeater unit shall be compatible at its AUI connector (if so equipped) as specified in Section 7 with the exception of the *signal_quality_error* message Test, 7.2.1.2.3, which shall not be implemented.

The MAUs associated with the repeater shall be as specified in Section 8 for type 10BASE5 or Section 10 for type 10BASE2 with the following restrictions:

(1) The MAU shall implement receive mode collision detect as defined in 8.3.1.5 or 10.4.1.5.

(2) The MAU shall not implement the *signal_quality_error* message Test function as defined in 8.2.1.1 and 10.3.1.1.

(3) The MAU shall not activate its Jabber function when operated under the worst case Jabber Lockup Protection condition as specified in 9.6.5.

9.4.2 Direct Cable Compatibility. The repeater set, which includes MAUs integrated with the repeater package (internal MAUs), may have any of the interfaces specified in the following subsections.

9.4.2.1 Direct Cable Attachment Compatibility. The repeater shall be compatible at its coaxial tap connector (if so equipped) as specified in 8.5.3 of the 10BASE5 standard. The MAUs associated with the repeater that are connected in this manner shall be subject to the restrictions of MAUs as specified in 9.4.1.

9.4.2.2 "N" Connector Compatibility. The repeater shall be compatible at its Type N connector (if so equipped) as specified in 8.5.0 of the 10BASE5 standard. The MAUs associated with the repeater that are connected in this manner shall be subject to the restrictions of MAUs as specified in 9.4.1.

9.4.2.3 BNC Compatibility. The repeater shall be compatible at its BNC connector (if so equipped) as specified in 10.6 of the 10BASE2 standard. The MAUs associated with the repeater that are connected in this manner shall be subject to the restrictions of MAUs as specified in 9.4.1.

9.4.3 IRL Compatibility. The compatibility interface for the IRL segment may be vendor dependent, or may conform to the specification in 9.4.3.2.

9.4.3.1 Vendor Dependent IRL. The budget allowances for the topology supported by the IRL shall ensure that the total network round trip delay requirement is met and the maximum collision frame size of 511 bits is not exceeded. (See 8.6.1 and 10.7.1.)

9.4.3.2 Vendor Independent Fiber-Optic IRL. A vendor independent fiber-optic IRL (FOIRL) provides a standard means of connecting two repeater units. It comprises a fiber-optic medium link segment, a fiber-optic MAU (FOMAU) at each end of the link segment, and if present, AU Interfaces. A vendor independent FOIRL is suitable for interconnecting coaxial segments, expecially segments located in different buildings.

The vendor independent FOMAU should be compatible at its fiber-optic medium interface as specified in 9.9. If a FOMAU contains an AU Interface, it shall be electrically and mechanically compatible at its AUI connector as specified in Section 7, with the exception of the *signal_quality_error* message Test, 7.2.1.2.3, which shall not be implemented.

9.5 Basic Functions

9.5.1 Repeater Set Network Properties. The repeater set shall be transparent to all network acquisition activity and to all DTEs. The repeater set shall not alter the basic fairness criterion for all DTEs to access the network or weigh it towards any DTE or group of DTEs regardless of network location. A repeater set shall not attempt to be a packet store and forward device.

Repeaters are not addressable. An addressable station on the network that controls a repeater is outside the scope of this standard.

9.5.2 Signal Amplification. The repeater set (including its associated or integral MAUs) shall ensure that the amplitude characteristics of the signals at the MAU outputs of the repeater set are within the tolerance of the specification for MAU outputs in 8.3.1.3 or 10.4.1.3. Therefore, any loss of signal-to-noise ratio due to cable loss and noise pickup is regained at the output of the repeater set as long as the incoming data is within the system specification.

9.5.3 Signal Symmetry. The repeater set shall ensure that the symmetry characteristics of the signals at the MAU outputs of the repeater set are within the tolerance of the specification for MAU outputs in 8.3.1.4 or 10.4.1.4. Therefore, any loss of symmetry due to MAUs and cable distortion is regained at the output of the repeater set.

9.5.4 Signal Retiming. The repeater unit shall ensure that the encoded data output from the repeater unit is within the jitter tolerance of a transmitting DTE as specified in 7.3. Therefore jitter cannot accumulate over multiple segments.

9.5.5 Data Handling. The repeater unit, when presented a packet at any of its ports, shall pass the data frame of said packet intact and without modification, subtraction, or addition to all other ports connected with the repeater unit. The only exceptions to this rule are when contention exists among any of the ports or when the receive port is partitioned as defined in 9.6.6. Between unpartitioned ports, the rules for collision handling (9.5.6) take precedence.

9.5.5.1 Start of Packet Propagation Delays. The start of packet propagation delay for a repeater set is the time delay between the first edge transition of the packet on its repeated from (input) port to the first edge transition of the packet on its repeated to (output) port (or ports).

For a repeater unit with AU Interface connectors at input and output ports, this time shall be less than or equal to 8 bit times.

For a repeater set with internal MAUs on both input and output ports, an additional 6.5 bit times delay for an input port MAU and 3.5 bit times delay for an output port MAU shall be allowed. This added delay does not include any dc rise time for the coaxial cable.

9.5.6 Collision Handling

9.5.6.1 Collision Presence. The repeater set shall implement the Collision Presence function using Receive Mode Collision Detection as specified for the media with which it is connected.

9.5.6.2 Jam Generation. If a collision is detected on any of the ports to which the repeater set is transmitting, the repeater set shall transmit a Jam to all of the ports to which it is connected. The Jam shall be transmitted in accordance with the Repeater Unit State Diagram in Fig 9-2 and shall be as specified in 4.2.3.2.4 with the further constraint that the first 62 bits transmitted to any port shall be a pattern of alternate 1's and 0's starting with the first bit transmitted as a 1.

9.5.6.3 Collision-Jam Propagation Delays. The start of collision propagation delay for a repeater set is the time delay between the first edge transition of the *signal_quality_error* signal on any of its ports to the first edge transition of the Jam on its (output) port (or ports).

For a repeater unit with AU Interface connectors at input and output ports, this time shall be less than or equal to 6.5 bit times.

For a repeater set with internal MAUs on both input and output ports, an additional allowance of 9 bit times delay for an input port MAU and 3.5 bit times delay for an output port MAU shall be made. This added delay does not include any dc rise time for the coaxial cable.

The cessation of Jam propagation delay for a repeater unit is the time delay between the input signals at its ports reaching a state such that Jam should end at a port and the last transition of Jam at that port. The states of the input signals that should cause Jam to end are covered in detail in the repeater state diagrams.

For a repeater unit with AU Interface connectors at input and output ports, this time shall be less than or equal to 5 bit times when not extending fragments. When extending fragments this delay may be longer as required by the fragment extension algorithm. See 9.6.4.

For a repeater set with internal MAUs on its input ports, an additional allowance of 0.5 bit time delay for DI and 20 bit times for *signal_quality_error* deassertion shall be made. For a repeater set with internal MAUs on its output ports, an additional allowance of 0.5 bit time delay shall be made. This added delay does not include any dc fall time for the coaxial cable.

9.5.6.4 Transmit Recovery Time. It is essential that the repeater unit not monitor a port for input for a short time after the repeater stops transmitting to that port. This recovery time prevents the repeater from receiving its own transmission as a new receive activity. The minimum recovery time allowable for a repeater is implementation dependent, but must be greater than the sum of the delays in the transmit and receive paths for the port. In all cases the recovery time must be less than 10 bit times from the last transition on the transmitting AU Interface.

9.5.6.5 Carrier Recovery Time. During a collision the *input_idle* signal is unreliable for short periods of time (bits) because of the possibility of signal cancellation on the collision segment. In order to prevent premature detection of the true end of the collision, the repeater unit must wait for data to become sensed from a port for a short time after *signal_quality_error* has gone inactive from that port. This recovery time prevents the repeater from prematurely ending a Jam on an active network. The minimum carrier recovery time allowable for a repeater is implementation dependent, but shall be greater than the CARRIER ON time after *signal_quality_error* is deasserted. In all cases the carrier recovery time shall be less than 4 bit times from the last transition on the AU Interface.

9.5.7 Electrical Isolation. Network segments that have different isolation and grounding requirements shall have those requirements provided by the port-to-port isolation of the repeater set.

9.6 Detailed Repeater Functions and State Diagrams. A precise algorithmic definition is given in this section, providing a complete procedural model for the operation of a repeater, in the form of state diagrams. Note that whenever there is any apparent ambiguity concerning the definition of repeater operation, the state diagrams should be consulted for the definitive statement.

The model presented in this section is intended as a primary specification of the functions to be provided by any repeater unit. It is important to distinguish, however, between the model and a real implementation. The model is optimized for simplicity and clarity of presentation, while any realistic implementation should place heavier emphasis on such constraints as efficiency and suitability to a particular implementation technology.

It is the functional behavior of any repeater unit implementation that shall match the standard, not the internal structure. The internal details of the procedural model are useful only to the extent that they help specify the external behavior clearly and precisely. For example, the model uses a separate Transmit Timer state machine for each port. However, in an actual implementation the hardware may be shared.

9.6.1 State Diagram Notation. The notation used in the state diagrams follows the conventions in 1.2.1, with the following additions:

The character ":" (colon) is a delimiter used to denote that a term assignment statement follows.

The character "⇐" denotes assignment of the value following the arrow to the term preceding the arrow.

Description of State Diagram Variables

Input/Output Variables

DataIn (X)
Status of DataIn input at port X.
Values: II = *input_idle* ; indicates no activity
-II ; indicates activity
Note that DataIn (X) may be undefined during collision but that it is a don't care in all instances when this is true.

CollIn (X)
Status of ControlIn input at port X.
Values: SQE = *signal_quality_error* ; indicates collision
-SQE ; indicates no collision

Out (X)
Type of output repeater is sourcing at port X.
Values: Idle ; Repeater is not transmitting
-Idle ; Repeater is transmitting Preamble Pattern or Data or Jam or TwoOnes.
Preamble Pattern ; Repeater is sourcing alternating 1's and 0's on port X.
Data ; Repeater is repeating data frame on port X.
Jam ; Repeater is sourcing Jam on port X.
TwoOnes ; Repeater is sourcing two consecutive manchester encoded ones on port X.

DisableOut(X)
Override of Out(X)
Values: ON = Disable repeater transmission regardless of value of Out(X).
-ON = Repeater transmission depends on the value of Out(X).

Port Variables

TT (X)
Transmit Timer. Indicates number of bits transmitted on port X
Values: Positive Integers

Inter Process Flags

AllDataSent
All received data frame bits have been sent.

Bit Transmitted
Indicates a bit has been transmitted by the repeater unit.

DataRdy
Indicates the Repeater has detected the Start of Frame Delimiter and is ready to send the received data. The search for Start of Frame Delimiter shall not begin before 15 bits have been received. Note, transmit and receive clock differences shall also be accommodated.

Tw1
Wait Timer for the end of transmit recovery time (see 9.5.6.4). It is started by StartTw1. Tw1Done is satisfied when the end of transmit recovery time is completed.

Tw2
Wait Timer for the end of carrier recovery time (see 9.5.6.5). It is started by StartTw2. Tw2Done is satisfied when the timer has expired.

Tw3
Wait Timer for length of continuous output (see 9.6.5). It is started by StartTw3. Tw3Done is satisfied when the timer has expired.

Tw4
Wait Timer for time to disable output for Jabber Lockup Protection (see 9.6.5). It is started by StartTw4. Tw4Done is satisfied when the timer has expired.

Port Functions

PORT(*Test*)
A function that returns the designation of a port passing the test condition. For example Port(CollIn=SQE) returns the designation: X for a port that has SQE true. If multiple ports meet the test condition, the port function will be assigned one and only one of the acceptable values.

Port Designation

Ports are referred to by number. Port information is obtained by replacing the X in the desired function with the number of the port of interest. Ports are referred to in general as follows:

ALL	Indicates all repeater ports are to be considered. All ports shall meet test conditions in order for the test to pass.
ANY	Indicates all ports are to be considered. One or more ports shall meet the test conditions in order for the test to pass.
ONLY1	Indicates all ports are to be considered. One, but not more than one, port shall meet the test condition in order for the test to pass.
X	Generic port designator. When X is used in a state diagram its value is local to that diagram and not global to the set of state diagrams.
N	Is defined by the Port function on exiting the IDLE state of Fig 9-2. It indicates a port that caused the exit from the IDLE state.
M	Is defined by the Port function on exiting the TRANSMIT COLLISION state of Fig 9-2. It indicates the only port where CollIn=SQE.
ALLXN	Indicates all ports except N should be considered. All ports considered shall meet the test conditions in order for the test to pass.
ALLXM	Indicates all ports except M should be considered. All ports considered shall meet the test conditions in order for the test to pass.
ANYXN	Indicates any port other than N meeting the test conditions shall cause the test to pass.
ANYXM	Indicates any port other than M meeting the test conditions shall cause the test to pass.

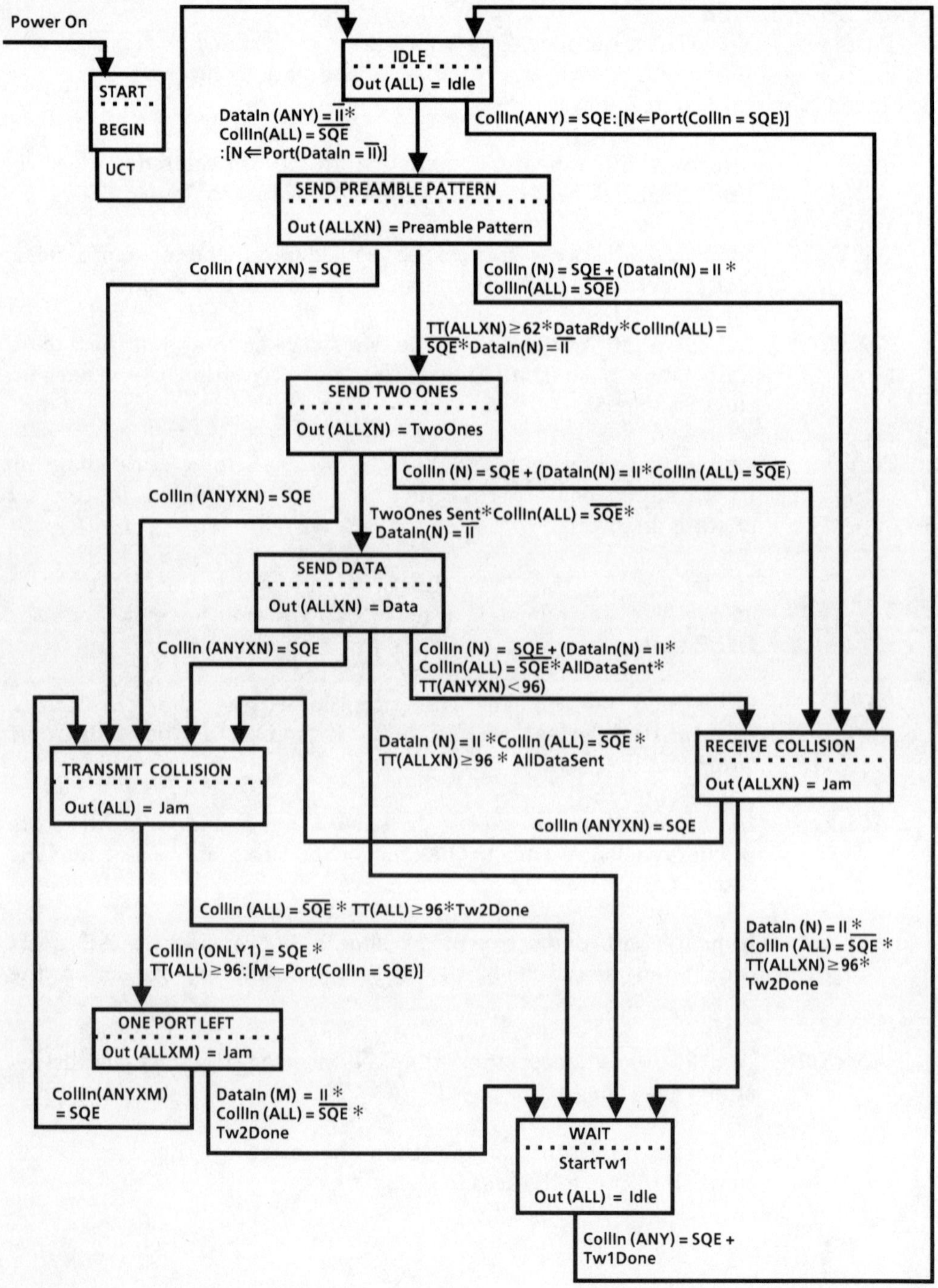

Fig 9-2
Repeater Unit State Diagram

Note: Output (X)=Idle in all instances unless specified otherwise.

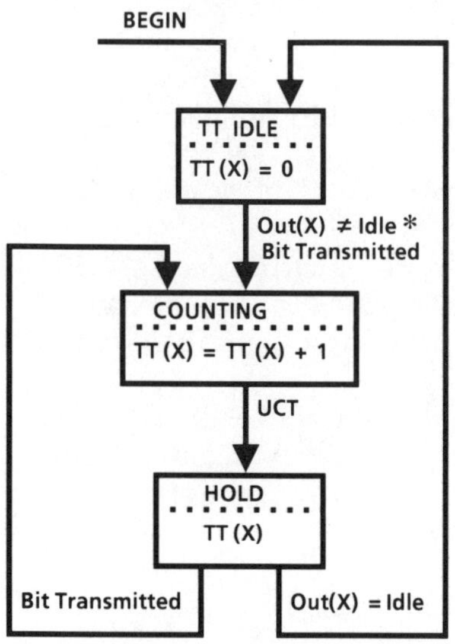

Fig 9-3
Transmit Timer State Diagram for Port X

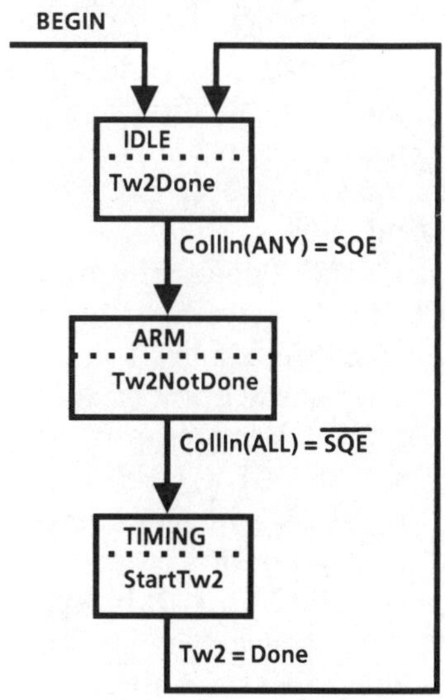

Fig 9-4
Tw2 State Diagram

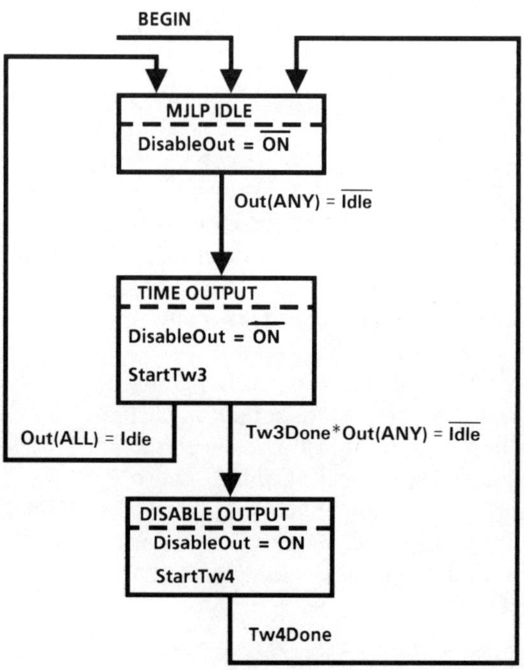

Fig 9-5
MAU Jabber Lockup Protection State Diagram

9.6.2 Data and Collision Handling. The repeater unit shall implement the CARRIER_ON function for all its ports. Upon detection of carrier from one port, the repeater unit shall repeat all received signals in the Data Frame from that port to the other port or ports.

The repeater unit data and collision handling algorithm shall be as defined in Fig 9-2.

9.6.3 Preamble Regeneration. The repeater unit shall output at least 56 bits of preamble followed by the Start Frame Delimiter. When the repeater unit must send more than 56 bits, the maximum length preamble pattern it shall send is the number received plus 6.

9.6.4 Fragment Extension. If the received bit sequence from CARRIER_ON to CARRIER_OFF is fewer than 96 bits in length including preamble, the repeater unit shall extend the output bit sequence with JAM such that the total number of bits output from the repeater unit shall equal 96.

9.6.5 MAU Jabber Lockup Protection. MAU Jabber Lockup Protection must operate as shown in the MAU Jabber Lockup Protection State diagram. The repeater unit shall interrupt its output if it has transmitted continuously for longer than 5 ms or 50 000 bit times -20%+50%. The repeater unit shall then, after 96 to 116 bit times (9.6 to 11.6 μs), reenable transmissions.

9.6.6 Auto Partitioning/Reconnection (Optional)

9.6.6.1 Overview. In large multi-segment networks it may be desirable that the repeater unit protect the network from some fault conditions that would halt all network communication. A potentially likely cause of this condition could be due to a cable break, a faulty connector, or a faulty or missing termination.

In order to isolate a faulty segment's collision activity from propagating through the network, the repeater unit may optionally implement an auto-partition algorithm and, on detection of the malfunction being cleared, an auto-reconnection algorithm.

9.6.6.2 Detailed Auto Partition/Reconnection Algorithm State Diagram. The repeater unit may optionally implement an auto partition/reconnection algorithm that protects the rest of the network from an open circuited segment. If the repeater unit provides this function, it shall conform to the state diagram of Fig 9-6.

The algorithm defined in Fig 9-6 shall isolate a segment from the network when one of the following two conditions has occurred on the segment: (1) when a consecutive collision count has been reached; or (2) when a single collision duration has exceeded a specific amount of time.

When a segment is partitioned, DataIn(X) and CollIn(X) from that segment are forced to II (input idle) and -SQE (no collision), respectively, so that activity on the port will not affect the repeater unit. Output from the repeater to the segment is not blocked.

The segment will be reinstated when the repeater has detected activity on the segment for more than the number of bits specified for Tw5 without incurring a collision.

9.6.6.2.1 Description of State Diagram Variables and Constants

Port Constants

CCLimit
The number of consecutive collisions which must occur before a segment is partitioned. The value shall be greater than 30.

Input/Output Variables

DIPresent(X)
Data in from the MAU on port X. (This input is gated by the Partition State Machine to produce DataIn(X) to the main state machine.)
Values: II = *input_idle* ; no activity
-II= Input not idle ; activity

CIPresent(X)
Control input from the MAU on port X. (This input is gated by the Partition State Machine to produce CollIn(X) to the main state machine.)
Values: SQE = *signal_quality_error* ; indicates collision
-SQE ; indicates no collision

Port Variables

CC(X)
Consecutive port collision count on a particular port X. Partitioning occurs on a terminal count of CCLimit being reached.
Values: Positive Integers up to a terminal count of CCLimit.

Inter Process Flags

Tw5
Wait Timer for length of packet without collision. Its value shall be between 450 and 560 bit times. It is started by StartTw5. Tw5Done is satisfied when the timer has expired.

Tw6
Wait Timer for excessive length of collision. Its value shall be between 1000 and 30 000 bit times. It is started by StartTw6. Tw6Done is satisfied when the timer has expired.

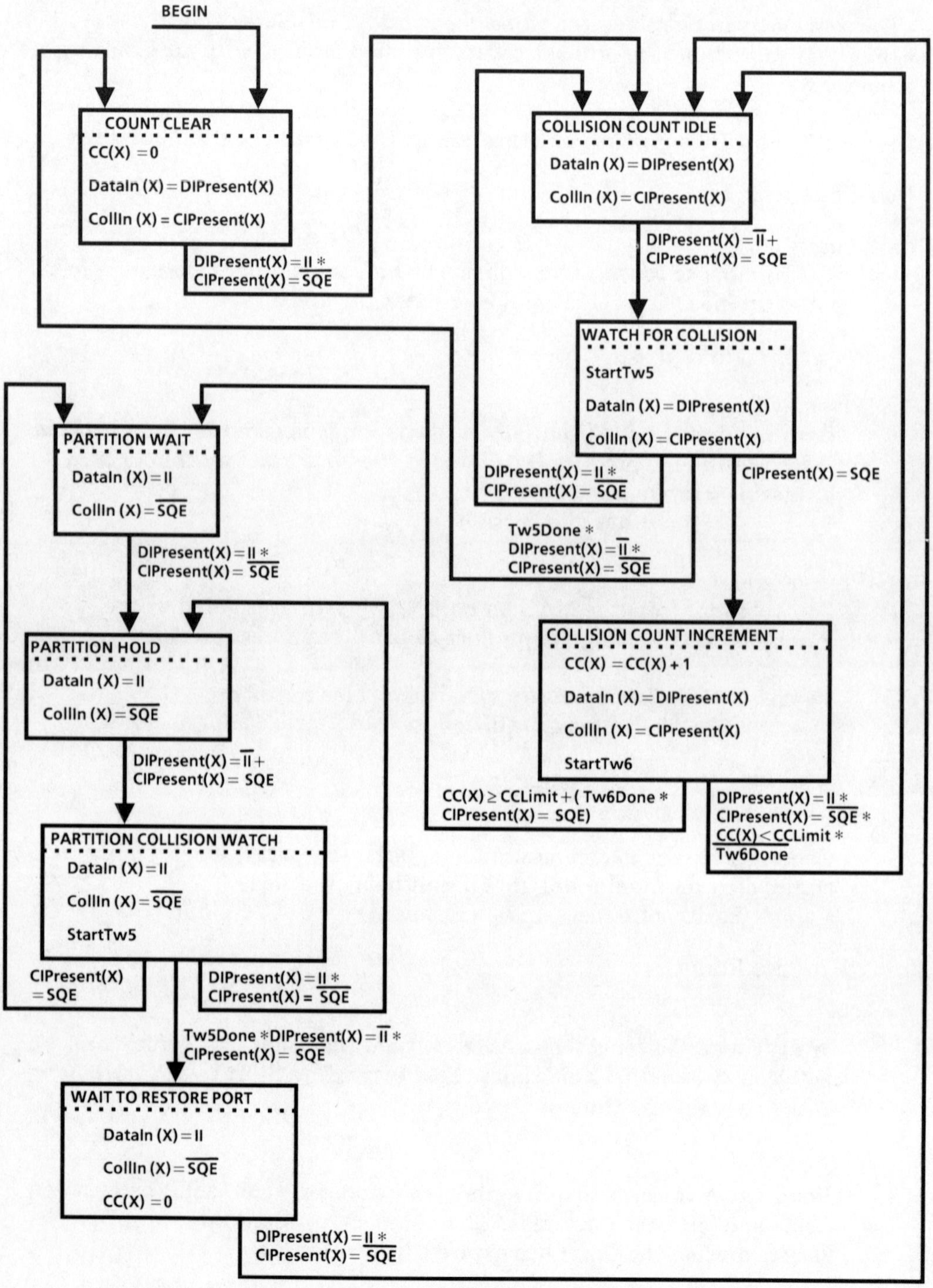

Fig 9-6
Partitioning State Diagram for Port X

9.7 Electrical Isolation. There are two electrical power distribution environments to be considered that require different electrical isolation properties.

Environment A — When a LAN or LAN segment, with all its associated interconnected equipment, is entirely contained within a single low-voltage power distribution system and within a single building.

Environment B — When a LAN crosses the boundary between separate power distribution systems or the boundaries of a single building.

The repeater unit shall comply with applicable local and national codes related to safety. See Annex [14].

9.7.1 Environment A Requirements. Attachment of network segments via repeaters (sets) possessing internal MAUs requires electrical isolation of 500 Vrms, 1 minute withstand, between the segment and the protective ground of the repeater unit.

For repeater ports that connect to external MAUs via an AU Interface, the requirement for isolation is encompassed within the isolation requirements of the basic MAU standard. (See 8.3.2.1 and 10.4.2.1.) The repeater unit shall not require any electrical isolation between exposed AU Interfaces or between exposed AU Interfaces and chassis ground of the repeater unit. No isolation boundary need therefore exist at any AUI compatible interface (that is "D" connector) provided by a repeater unit.

9.7.2 Environment B Requirements. The attachment of network segments, which cross environment A boundaries, requires electrical isolation of 1500 V rms, 1 minute withstand, between each segment and all other attached segments and also the protective ground of the repeater unit.

It is recommended that this isolation be provided by the use of external MAUs connected by AU Interfaces. If internal MAUs are used the segments shall be installed such that it is not possible for an equipment user to touch the trunk cable screen or signal conductor. A repeater of this variety requires professional installation.

The requirements for interconnected coaxial cable/electrically conducting LAN segments that are partially or fully external to a single building environment may require additional protection against lightning strike hazards. Such requirements are beyond the scope of this standard. It is recommended that the above situation be handled by the use of a nonelectrically conducting IRL (for example Fiber-Optic).

It is assumed that any nonelectrically conducting segments will provide sufficient isolation within that media to satisfy the isolation requirements of environment B.

9.8 Reliability. A 2 port repeater set shall be designed to provide a Mean Time Between Failure (MTBF) of at least 50 000 hours of continuous operation without causing a communication failure among stations attached to the network medium. Repeater sets with more than two ports shall add no more than 3.46×10^{-6} failures per hour for each additional port.

The repeater set electronics shall be designed to minimize the probability of component failures within the repeater electronics that prevent communication among the other MAUs on the individual coaxial cable segments. Connectors and other passive components comprising the means of connecting the repeater to the coaxial cable shall be designed to minimize the probability of total network failure.

9.9 Medium Attachment Unit and Baseband Medium Specification for a Vendor Independent Fiber Optic Inter Repeater Link

9.9.1 Scope

9.9.1.1 Overview. A vendor independent FOIRL provides a standard means for connecting only two repeater units. It thus extends the network length and topology beyond that which could be achieved by interconnecting coax segments via repeater sets only, as defined in 8.6 or 10.7. A vendor independent FOIRL is particularly suited for interconnecting coax segments located in different buildings. The FOMAU described in this document is not intended for use in connecting DTEs.

In particular, this section defines the following:

(1) The functional, optical, electrical, and mechanical characteristics of a fiber-optic MAU (FOMAU) suitable for interfacing to a repeater unit, either directly (FOMAU and repeater unit integrated into a single package) or via an AUI.

(2) One specific optical fiber medium for connecting only two FOMAUs.

A schematic of the vendor independent FOIRL and its relationship to the repeater unit is shown in Fig 9-7. The vendor independent FOIRL comprises an optical fiber cable link segment, a vendor independent FOMAU at each end of the link segment and, if present, AU Interfaces.

The purpose of this specification is to enable interoperability of FOMAUs that originate from different manufacturers, thereby facilitating the development of simple and inexpensive inter repeater links. To satisfy this objective, the FOMAU has the following general characteristics:

(1) Enables coupling the repeater unit PLS directly, or by way of the AUI, to the explicit baseband optical fiber cable link segment defined in this section of the standard.

(2) Supports signaling at a data rate of 10 Mb/s.

(3) Provides for driving up to 1000 m of an optical fiber cable link segment.

(4) Operates indistinguishably from a repeater set MAU, as defined in Section 8 or 10, when viewed from the AU Interface.

(5) Supports 10BASE5 and 10BASE2 system configurations as defined in Sections 8 and 10 of this standard.

(6) Allows integration of the FOMAU into a single package with the repeater unit, thereby eliminating the need for an AUI.

The implementation may incorporate additional features, for example, those

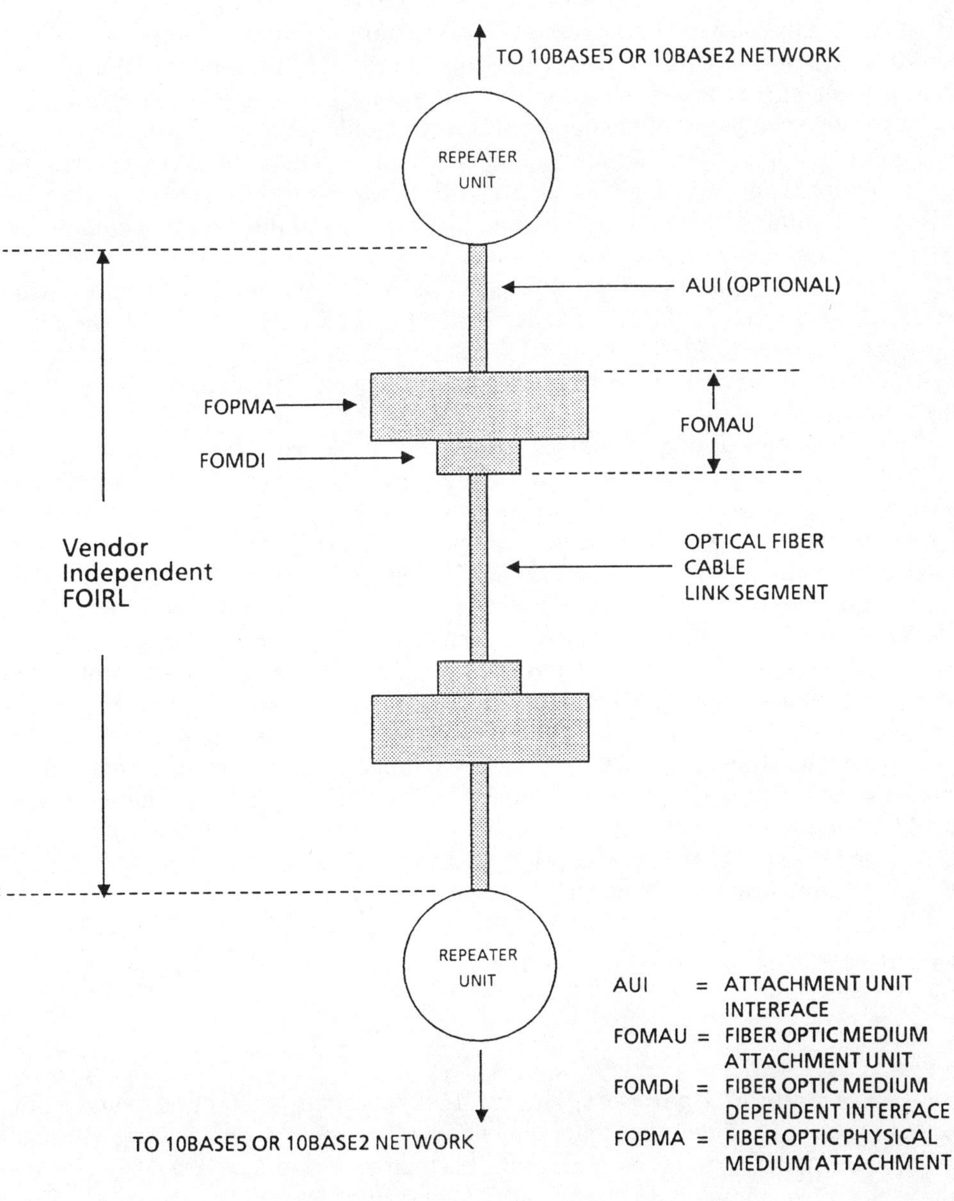

Fig 9-7
Schematic of the Vendor Independent FOIRL and Its Relationship to the Repeater Unit

that allow compatibility with vendor dependent FOMAUs, as in 9.4.3.1. The means to support these features are beyond the scope of this section.

9.9.1.2 Application Perspective: FOMAU and MEDIUM Objectives. This section states the broad objectives underlying the vendor independent FOIRL specification defined throughout this section of the standard. These are as follows:

(1) Provide the physical means for connecting only two repeater units.

(2) Define a physical interface for the vendor independent FOMAU component of the vendor independent FOIRL that can be implemented independently among different manufacturers of hardware and achieve the intended level of compatibility when interconnected in a common IRL.

(3) Provide a communication channel capable of high bandwidth and low bit error rate performance. The resultant mean bit error rate of the FOIRL should be less than one part in 10^{10}.

(4) Provide a means to prevent packet transmission through an FOIRL when full duplex operation is disrupted.

9.9.1.3 Compatibility Considerations. All implementations of the vendor independent FOMAU shall be compatible at the AUI (when implemented) and FOMDI.

This standard provides one explicit optical fiber cable link segment specification for the interconnection of only two FOMAU devices. The medium itself, the functional capability of the FOMAU, and the AUI are defined to provide the highest possible level of compatibility among devices designed by different manufacturers. Designers are free to implement circuitry within the FOMAU in an application dependent manner provided the FOMDI and AUI (when implemented) are satisfied.

9.9.1.4 Relationship to AUI. A close relationship exists between this section and Section 7. This section specifies all of the physical medium parameters, all of the FOPMA logical functions residing in the FOMAU, and references the AUI defined in Section 7 with the exception of the *signal_quality_error* message Test of 7.2.1.2.3, subparagraph 3, which shall not be implemented.

NOTE: The specification of a FOMAU component requires the use of both this section and Section 7 for the AUI specifications.

9.9.1.5 Mode of Operation. The FOMAU functions as a direct connection between the optical fiber cable link segment and the repeater unit. During collision-free operation, data from the repeater unit is transmitted into the FOMAU's transmit optical fiber and all data in the FOMAU's receive optical fiber are transmitted to the repeater unit.

9.9.2 FOMAU Functional Specifications. The FOMAU component provides the means by which signals on the three AUI signal circuits are coupled:

(1) from the repeater unit into the FOMAU's transmit optical fiber, and

(2) from the FOMAU's receive optical fiber to the repeater unit.

To achieve this basic objective, the FOMAU component contains the following functional capabilities to handle message flow between the repeater unit and the optical fiber cable link segment:

(1) *Transmit Function* : The ability to transmit serial data bit streams into the FOMAU's transmit optical fiber from the attached repeater unit.

(2) *Receive Function* : The ability to receive serial data bit streams from the FOMAU's receive optical fiber and transmit them to the attached repeater unit.

(3) *Collision Presence Function* : The ability to detect, and report to the attached repeater unit, an FOIRL collision.

(4) *Jabber Function* : The ability to automatically interrupt the Transmit Function and inhibit an abnormally long output data stream.

(5) *Low Light Level Detection Function* : The ability to automatically interrupt the Receive Function and inhibit the reception of signals from the FOMAU's receive optical fiber that could result in abnormally high BERs.

9.9.2.1 Transmit Function Requirements. At the start of a packet transmission into the FOMAU's transmit optical fiber, no more than two bits (two full bit cells) of information may be received from the DO circuit and not transmitted into the FOMAU's transmit optical fiber. In addition, it is permissible for the first bit sent to contain encoded phase violations or invalid data. All successive bits of the packet shall be transmitted into the FOMAU's transmit optical fiber and shall exhibit:

(1) no more edge jitter than that given by the sum of the worst-case edge jitter components specified in 7.4.3.6, 7.5.2.1, and 9.9.4.1.7, and

(2) the levels and waveforms specified in 9.9.4.1.

The FOMAU DO circuit shall comply with the AUI specification for receivers given in 7.4.2. The FOMAU's DI circuit driver shall comply with the AUI specification for drivers given in 7.4.1.

The steady-state propagation delay between the DO circuit receiver input and the FOMAU's transmit optical fiber input shall not exceed one-half of a bit cell. It is recommended that the designer provide an implementation in which a minimum threshold level is required in the DO circuit to establish a transmit bit stream.

The higher optical power level transmitted into the FOMAU's transmit optical fiber shall be defined as the low (LO) logic state on the optical fiber link segment. There shall be no logical signal inversions between the DO circuit and the FOMAU's transmit optical fiber, as specified in 9.9.4.1.5.

The difference in the start-up delay (bit loss plus invalid bits plus steady-state propagation delay), as distinct from the absolute start-up delays, between any two packets that are separated by 9.6 μs or less shall not exceed 2 bit cells.

The FOMAU shall loop back a packet received from the DO circuit into the DI circuit. At the start of a packet transmission, no more than five bits of information may be received from the DO circuit and not transmitted into the DI circuit. It is permissible for the first bit sent to contain encoded phase violations or invalid data. All successive bits of the packet shall be transmitted into the DI circuit and shall exhibit no more edge jitter than that specified for signals transmitted into the DI circuit by the Receive Function, as specified in 9.9.2.2. The steady-state propagation delay between the DO circuit receiver input and the DI circuit driver output for such signals shall not exceed one bit cell. There shall be no logical signal inversions between the DO circuit and the DI circuit during collision-free transmission.

When the DO circuit has gone idle after a packet has been transmitted into the FOMAU's transmit optical fiber, the FOMAU shall not activate the Collision Presence Function so as not to send the *signal_quality_error* message Test of 7.2.1.2.3, subparagraph 3, to the repeater unit.

During the idle state of the DO circuit, the Transmit Function shall output into the transmit optical fiber an optical idle signal as specified in 9.9.4.1.4. The transmitted optical signals shall exhibit the optical power levels specified in 9.9.4.1.8. At the end of a packet transmission, the first optical idle signal pulse transition to the higher optical power level must occur no sooner than 400 ns and no later than 2100 ns after the packet's last transition to the lower optical power level. This first optical pulse must meet the timing requirements of 9.9.4.1.4.

The Transmit Function shall not introduce extraneous optical signals into the FOMAU's transmit optical fiber under normal operating conditions, including powering-up or powering-down of the FOMAU.

9.9.2.2 Receive Function Requirements. At the start of a packet reception from the FOMAU's receive optical fiber, no more than two bits (two full bit cells) of information may be received from the FOMAU's receive optical fiber and not transmitted into the DI circuit. It is permissible for the first bit transmitted into the DI circuit to contain encoded phase violations or invalid data. All successive bits of the packet shall be transmitted into the DI circuit and shall exhibit:

(1) the levels and waveforms specified in 7.4.1, and

(2) no more edge jitter than that given by the sum of the worst-case edge jitter components specified in 7.4.3.6, 7.5.2.1, 9.9.4.1.7, 9.9.4.2.2, and 9.9.5.1.

The steady-state propagation delay between the output of the FOMAU's receive optical fiber and the output of the DI circuit driver shall not exceed one-half of a bit cell. There shall be no logical signal inversions between the FOMAU's receive optical fiber and the DI circuit during collision-free operation, as specified in 9.9.4.2.3.

The difference in the start-up delay (bit loss plus invalid bits plus steady-state propagation delay), as distinct from the absolute start-up delays, between any two packets that are separated by 9.6 μs or less shall not exceed 2 bit cells.

The Receive Function shall not introduce extraneous signals into the DI circuit under normal operating conditions, including powering-up or powering-down of the FOMAU.

9.9.2.3 Collision Presence Function Requirements. The signal presented to the CI circuit in the absence of an SQE signal shall be the IDL signal.

The signal presented to the CI circuit during the presence of a collision shall be the CSO signal, a periodic pulse waveform of frequency 10 MHz + 25%, - 15% with pulse transitions that are no less than 35 ns and no greater than 70 ns apart at the zero crossing points. This signal shall be presented to the CI circuit no more than 3.5 bit times after the simultaneous appearance of signals at both the input of the FOMAU's transmit optical fiber and the output of the FOMAU's receive optical fiber. This signal shall be deasserted no earlier than 4.5 bit times and no later than 7 bit times after the above defined collision condition ceases to exist.

During a collision, if a packet is received at the DO circuit before a packet is received at the FOMAU's receive optical fiber, then only the packet received at the DO circuit shall be transmitted into the DI circuit, as specified in 9.9.2.1. Conversely, if during a collision a packet is received at the FOMAU's receive optical fiber before a packet is received at the DO circuit, then only the packet received at the FOMAU's receive optical fiber shall be transmitted into the DI circuit, as specified in 9.9.2.2. In the event of both packets being received at their respective ports within 3.5 bit times of each other, then either one, but only one, of the packets shall be selected to be transmitted into the DI circuit.

The Collision Function shall not introduce extraneous signals into the CI circuit under normal operating conditions, including powering-up or powering-down of the FOMAU.

9.9.2.4 Jabber Function Requirements. The FOMAU shall have the capability, as defined in Fig 9-9, to interrupt a transmission from the repeater unit that exceeds a time duration determined by the FOMAU. This time duration shall not be less than 20 ms or more than 150 ms. If the packet being transmitted is still being transmitted after the specified time duration, the FOMAU shall activate the Jabber Function by:

(1) first inhibiting the transmission of bits from its DO circuit into its transmit optical fiber,

(2) then transmitting into its transmit optical fiber the optical idle signal specified in 9.9.4.1.4, and

(3) presenting the CS0 signal to the CI circuit.

Once the error condition has been cleared, the FOMAU shall reset the Jabber Function and present the IDL signal to the CI circuit:

(1) on power reset, and

(2) optionally, automatically after a continuous period of 0.5 s $\pm$ 50% of inactivity on the DO circuit.

The FOMAU shall not activate its Jabber Function when operated under the worst-case Jabber Lockup Protection condition specified in 9.6.5.

When both the Jabber Function and the Low Light Level Detection Function (see 9.9.2.5) have been activated, the Jabber Function shall override the Low Light Level Detection Function.

9.9.2.5 Low Light Level Detection Function Requirements. The FOMAU shall have a low light level detection capability, as defined in Fig 9-10, whereby it shall interrupt the reception of both the optical idle signal and packets from the FOMAU's receive optical fiber when reliable reception can no longer be assured. This error condition shall not be activated if the peak optical power level at the output of the FOMAU's receive optical fiber exceeds -27 dBm. It shall be activated before the peak optical power level at the output of the FOMAU's receive optical fiber has fallen to a level that is lower than the peak optical power level that corresponds to a BER = 10^{-10} for the FOMAU under consideration. Once this error condition has been activated, the FOMAU shall, no earlier than 30 bit times and no later than 200 bit times:

(1) Disable its Receive Function, so that the transmission of bits from its receive optical fiber to the DI circuit is inhibited.

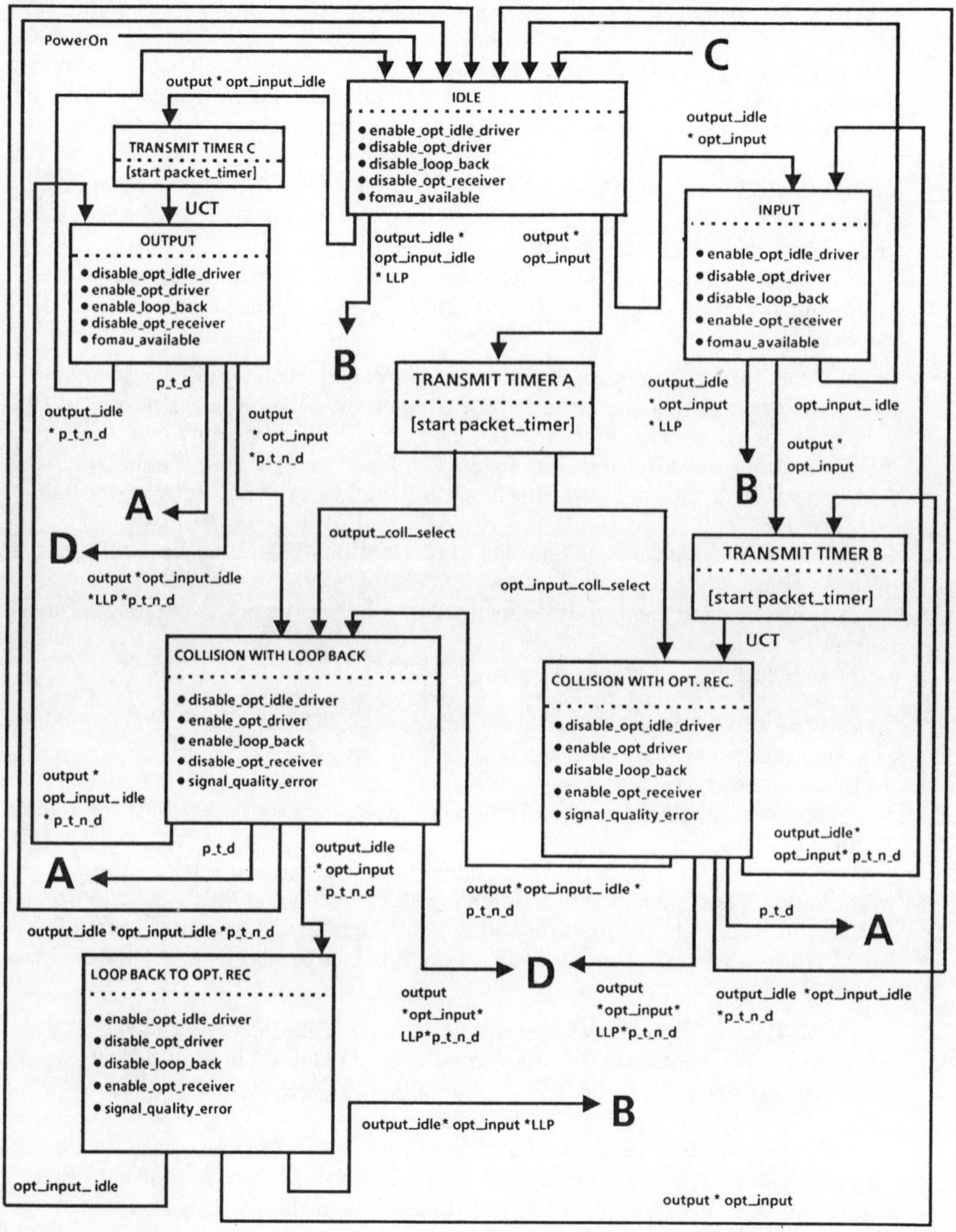

Fig 9-8
FOMAU Transmit, Receive and Collision Functions State Diagrams

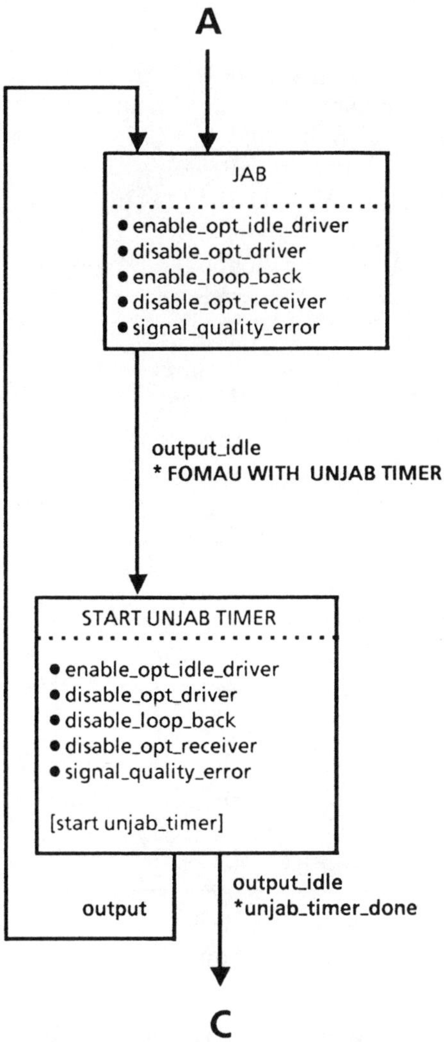

Fig 9-9
FOMAU Jabber Function State Diagram

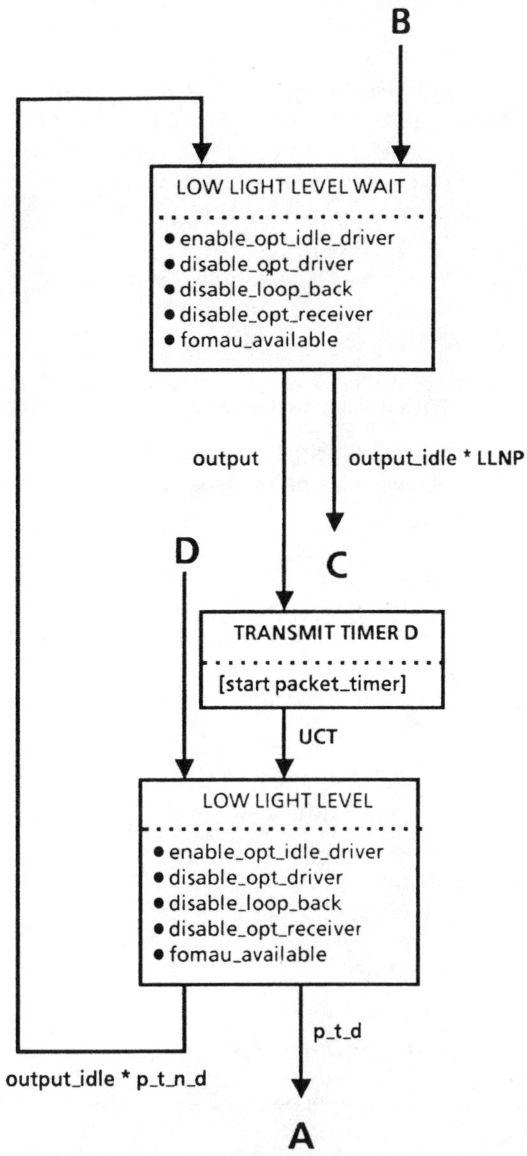

Fig 9-10
Low Light Level Detection Function State Diagram

(2) Assure that only the optical idle signal is transmitted into its transmit optical fiber irrespective of the state of the DO circuit.

(3) Disable its Transmit Function during the period of time that the FOMAU recognizes the presence of a packet on the DO circuit such that the transmission of the packet from the DO circuit into the DI circuit is inhibited.

Once this error condition has been cleared, the FOMAU shall return automatically to its normal mode of operation within 40 bit times once the DO circuit is in the idle state.

When both the Jabber Function (see 9.9.2.4) and the Low Light Level Detection Function have been activated, the Jabber Function shall override the Low Light Level Detection Function.

NOTE: It is recommended that, for diagnostic purposes, the status of the Low Light Level Detection Function be indicated on the exterior of the FOMAU package.

9.9.2.6 Repeater Unit to FOMAU Physical Layer Messages. The following messages can be received by the FOMAU physical layer entities from the repeater unit:

Message	Circuit	Signal	Meaning
output	DO	CD1,CD0	Output information
output_idle	DO	IDL	No data to be output

9.9.2.7 FOMAU Physical Layer to Repeater Unit Messages. The following messages can be sent by the FOMAU physical layer entities to the repeater unit:

Message	Circuit	Signal	Meaning
input	DI	CD1,CD0	Input information
input_idle	DI	IDL	No information to be input
fomau_available	CI	IDL	FOMAU is available for output
signal_quality_error	CI	CS0	Collision or error detected by FOMAU

9.9.2.7.1 *input* Message. The FOMAU physical layer sends an *input* message to the repeater unit when the FOMAU has a bit of data to send to the repeater unit. The physical realization of the *input* message is a CD0 or CD1 sent by the FOMAU to the repeater unit on the DI circuit. The FOMAU sends CD0 if the input bit is a zero, or CD1 if the input bit is a one. No retiming of the CD1 or CD0 signals takes place within the FOMAU.

9.9.2.7.2 *input_idle* Message. The FOMAU physical layer sends an *input_idle* message to the repeater unit when the FOMAU does not have data to send to the repeater unit. The physical realization of the *input_idle* message is the IDL signal sent by the FOMAU to the repeater unit on the DI circuit.

9.9.2.7.3 *fomau_available* Message. The FOMAU physical layer sends the *fomau_available* message to the repeater unit when the FOMAU is available for output, and when the FOMAU has activated the Low Light Level Detection Function in accordance with the Low Light Level Detection Function Requirements of 9.9.2.5 and Fig 9-10. The *fomau_available* message shall be sent by a FOMAU that is prepared to output data. The physical realization of the *fomau_available* message is an IDL signal sent by the FOMAU to the repeater unit on the CI circuit.

9.9.2.7.4 *signal_quality_error* Message. The *signal_quality_error* message shall be implemented in the following fashion:

(1) When the FOMAU has completed the transmission of a packet into its transmit optical fiber, it shall not send any *signal_quality_error* message Test sequence.

(2) The simultaneous appearance of packets at both the input of a FOMAU's transmit optical fiber and the output of its receive optical fiber shall cause the *signal_quality_error* message to be sent by the FOMAU to the repeater unit.

(3) When the FOMAU has activated the Jabber Function, it shall send the *signal_quality_error* message in accordance with the Jabber Function Requirements of 9.9.2.4 and Fig 9-9.

The physical realization of the *signal_quality_error* message is the CS0 signal sent by the FOMAU to the repeater unit on the CI circuit.

The FOMAU is required to assert the *signal_quality_error* message at the appropriate times whenever the FOMAU is powered and not just when the repeater unit is providing output data.

9.9.2.8 FOMAU State Diagrams. The state diagrams Figs 9-8, 9-9, and 9-10 depict the full set of allowed FOMAU state functions relative to the control circuits of the repeater unit/FOMAU interface for FOMAUs. Messages used in these state diagrams are explained below:

(1) *enable_opt_driver* : Activates the path employed during normal operation to cause the FOMAU transmitter to impress the packet data received from the DO circuit into the FOMAU's transmit optical fiber.

(2) *disable_opt_driver* : Deactivates the path employed during normal operation to cause the FOMAU transmitter to impress the packet data received from the DO circuit into the FOMAU's transmit optical fiber.

(3) *enable_opt_idle_driver* : Causes the FOMAU transmitter to impress the optical idle signal into the FOMAU's transmit optical fiber.

(4) *disable_opt_idle_driver* : Causes the FOMAU to stop transmitting the optical idle signal into the FOMAU's transmit optical fiber.

(5) *enable_loop_back* : Activates the path employed during normal operation to cause the FOMAU Transmit Function to impress the packet data received from the DO circuit into the DI circuit.

(6) *disable_loop_back* : Deactivates the path employed during normal operation to cause the FOMAU Transmit Function to impress the packet data received from the DO circuit into the DI circuit.

(7) *enable_opt_receiver* : Activates the path employed during normal operation to cause the FOMAU to impress the packet data received from the FOMAU's receive optical fiber into the DI circuit.

(8) *disable_opt_receiver* : Deactivates the path employed during normal operation to cause the FOMAU to impress the packet data received from the FOMAU's receive optical fiber into the DI circuit.

(9) [*start_packet_timer*] : Starts a timing function that is used to monitor the amount of time the FOMAU is transmitting a packet into the transmit optical fiber. The timing function is maintained as long as *output* is true and is stopped on the transition to *output_idle* true. The term *packet_timer_done* is satisfied when the timing function has run to expiration (see 9.9.2.4).

(10) [*start_unjab_timer*] : Starts a timing function that is used to monitor the amount of time that the Jabber error condition has been clear. The timing function is maintained as long as *output_idle* is true and is stopped on the transition to *output* true. The term *unjab_timer_done* is satisfied when the timing function has run to expiration (see 9.9.2.4).

(11) *opt_input* : Signifies that a packet is present at the FOMAU's receive optical fiber.

(12) *opt_input_idle* : Signifies that a packet is no longer present at the FOMAU's receive optical fiber.

(13) *opt_input_coll_select* : Signifies that, during a collision, a packet has been received at the DO circuit within 3.5 bit times of a packet being received at the FOMAU's receive optical fiber, and that only the packet received at the FOMAU's receive optical fiber is to be transmitted into the DI circuit.

(14) *output_coll_select* : Signifies that, during a collision, a packet has been received at the DO circuit within 3.5 bit times of a packet being received at the FOMAU's receive optical fiber, and that only the packet received at the DO circuit is to be transmitted into the DI circuit.

The following abbreviations have been used in Figs 9-8, 9-9, and 9-10:

(1) LLP = Low Light Level Condition present
(2) LLNP = Low Light Level Condition not present
(3) p_t_d = *packet_timer_done*
(4) p_t_n_d = *packet_timer_not_done*
(5) * = logical AND operator

NOTE: Figs 9-8, 9-9, and 9-10 must all be considered together.

9.9.3 FOMAU Electrical Characteristics

9.9.3.1 Electrical Isolation. Electrical isolation shall be provided between FOMAU's attached to the FOIRL by the optical fiber cable link segment. There shall be no conducting path between the optical medium connector plug and any conducting element within the optical fiber cable link segment. This isolation shall withstand at least one of the following electrical strength tests:

(1) 1500 V, rms at 50 to 60 Hz for 60 s, applied as specified in 5.3.2 of IEC Publication 950 [8].

(2) 2250 V dc for 60 s, applied as specified in 5.3.2 of IEC Publication 950 [8].

(3) A sequence of ten 2400 V impulses of alternating polarity, applied at intervals of not less than 1 s. The shape of the impulses shall be 1.2/50 μs (1.2 μs virtual front time, 50 μs virtual time of half value), as defined in IEC Publication 60 [11].

There shall be no isolation breakdown, as defined in 5.3.2 of IEC Publication 950 [8], during the test. The resistance after the test shall be at least 2 MΩ, measured at 500 V dc.

NOTE: Although isolation is provided by the optical fiber cable link segment, it is recommended that the normal noise immunity provided by common-mode isolation on the AUI be retained.

9.9.3.2 Power Consumption. The current drawn by the FOMAU shall not exceed 0.5 A when powered by the AUI source. The FOMAU shall be capable of operating from all possible voltage sources as supplied by the repeater unit (7.5.2.5 and 7.5.2.6) through the resistance of all permissible AUI cables. The surge current drawn by the FOMAU on power-up shall not exceed 5 A peak for a period of 10 ms. In addition, the FOMAU shall be capable of powering-up from 0.5 A current limited sources.

It is permissible as an option to provide a separate power source for the FOMAU. If a separate power source is implemented, provision will be made to assure that power shall under no circumstances be sourced on pin 13 (Circuit VP) of the AUI.

The FOMAU shall be labeled externally to identify the maximum value of power supply current required by the device when the AUI is implemented.

The FOMAU shall not introduce into the FOMAU transmit optical fiber or onto the DI or CI circuits of the AUI any extraneous signal on routine power-up or power-down under normal operating conditions.

The FOMAU shall be fully functional no later than 0.5 s after power is applied to it.

9.9.3.3 Reliability. The FOMAU shall be designed to provide a Mean Time Between Failure (MTBF) of at least 200 000 hours of operation without causing a communication failure among DTEs attached to the network. The FOMAU electronics shall be designed to minimize the probability of component failures within the FOMAU that prevent communication among other MAUs on the 10BASE5 and 10BASE2 segments. Connectors and other passive means of connection shall be designed to minimize the probability of total network failure.

9.9.3.4 FOMAU/Repeater Unit Electrical Characteristics. The electrical characteristics of the driver and receiver components connected to the AUI cable shall be identical to those specified in Section 7.

9.9.3.5 FOMAU/Repeater Unit Mechanical Connection. The FOMAU, if it implements the AUI, shall be provided with a 15-pin male connector, as specified in the AUI specification of Section 7.

9.9.4 FOMAU/Optical Medium Interface

9.9.4.1 Transmit Optical Parameters

9.9.4.1.1 Wavelength. The center wavelength of the optical source emission shall be between 790 nm and 860 nm.

9.9.4.1.2 Spectral Width. The spectral width of the optical source shall be less than 75 nm full-width half-maximum (FWHM).

9.9.4.1.3 Optical Modulation. The optical modulation during packet transmission shall be on-off keying of the optical source power. The minimum extinction ratio shall be 13 dB.

9.9.4.1.4 Optical Idle Signal. During the idle state of the DO circuit, the Transmit Function shall input into the FOMAU's transmit optical fiber an optical idle signal. This signal shall consist of a periodic pulse waveform of frequency 1 MHz + 25%, - 15% with a duty cycle ratio between 45/55 and 55/45.

9.9.4.1.5 Transmit Optical Logic Polarity. The higher optical power level transmitted into the FOMAU's transmit optical fiber shall correspond to the low (LO) logic state (see 7.4.2.1) of the AUI DO circuit.

9.9.4.1.6 Optical Rise and Fall Times. The optical rise and fall times of the FOMAU shall be no more than 10 ns from the 10% to the 90% levels. There shall be no more than 3 ns difference between the rise and fall times.

9.9.4.1.7 Transmit Optical Pulse Edge Jitter. The additional edge jitter introduced by the FOMAU from the input of the DO circuit receiver to the output of the electro-optic source shall be no more than 2 ns. The jitter measured at the input of the DO circuit receiver shall be measured at the zero crossing points as determined from the previous 16 or more transitions in any valid bit stream. The jitter measured at the output of the electro-optic source shall be measured at the power level median of the optical waveform's upper and lower power levels as determined from the previous 16 or more transitions in any valid optical bit stream.

9.9.4.1.8 Peak Coupled Optical Power. At the beginning of the FOMAU's lifetime, the measured peak optical power coupled into the FOMAU's transmit optical fiber, when terminated with an optical connector as specified in 9.9.5.2, shall be -12 dBm $\pm$ 2 dB when referenced to an optical fiber of nominal dimension of 62.5 μm core diameter and 0.275 nominal numerical aperture. The peak optical power shall be measured in the steady state and the measurement shall be independent of optical pulse ringing effects. Peak optical overshoot shall not exceed 10%.

NOTE: The source is allocated an aging margin of 3 dB over its operating lifetime. Thus, with respect to an optical fiber of nominal dimension of 62.5 μm core diameter and 0.275 nominal numerical aperture, the minimum launch peak power at the end of life is -17 dBm and the maximum initial launch peak power is -10 dBm. The variation in the peak coupled optical power into any of the optical fibers specified in 9.9.5.1 is $\pm$ 1 dB with respect to the above-mentioned nominal optical fiber. Hence, with respect to any of the optical fibers specified in 9.9.5.1, the minimum possible launch peak power at the end of life is -18 dBm and the maximum possible initial launch peak power is -9 dBm. The start of life minimum possible launch peak power is then -15 dBm.

9.9.4.2 Receive Optical Parameters

9.9.4.2.1 Receive Peak Optical Power Range. The BER shall be $< 10^{-10}$ for peak optical powers at the output of the FOMAU's receive optical fiber between -27 dBm and -9 dBm.

9.9.4.2.2 Receive Optical Pulse Edge Jitter. The additional edge jitter introduced by the FOMAU from the input of the opto-electric detector to the output of the DI circuit driver shall be no more than 4 ns. The jitter measured at the input of the opto-electric receiver shall be measured at the power level median of the optical waveform's upper and lower power levels as determined from the previous 16 or more transitions in any valid optical bit stream. The jitter measured at the output of the DI circuit driver shall be measured at the zero crossing points as determined from the previous 16 or more transitions in any valid bit stream. This requirement shall apply when the optical receive peak power level is in the range -27 dBm to -9 dBm.

9.9.4.2.3 Receive Optical Logic Polarity. The low (LO) logic state (see 7.4.2.1) on the DI circuit shall correspond to the presence of the higher optical power level at the output of the FOMAU's receive optical fiber.

9.9.5 Characteristics of the Optical Fiber Cable Link Segment. The optical fiber cable link segment is a length of optical fiber cable containing two optical fibers, as specified in 9.9.5.1, and comprising one or more optical fiber cable sections and their means of interconnection. Each optical fiber is terminated at each end in the optical connector plug specified in 9.9.5.2. The two optical fibers correspond to the FOMAU's transmit and receive optical fibers.

9.9.5.1 Optical Fiber Medium. The FOMAU can operate with a variety of optical fiber sizes, for example, 50/125 μm, 62.5/125 μm, 85/125 μm, 100/140 μm. To ensure interoperability of FOMAUs that originate from different manufacturers:

(1) The two cabled optical fibers contained in the optical fiber cable link segment shall satisfy the following optical fiber parameters:

(a) core diameter	: 62.5 ± 3 μm
(b) cladding diameter	: 125 ± 3 μm
(c) core/cladding concentricity error	: $\leq 6\%$
(d) core noncircularity	: $\leq 6\%$
(e) cladding noncircularity	: $\leq 2\%$
(f) numerical aperture	: 0.275 ± 0.015 (per IEC method C-11 in IEC Publication 793-1 [12])

and

(2) The optical fiber cable link segment shall have an attenuation less than or equal to 8 dB and a bandwidth greater than or equal to 150 MHz.

In order to satisfy the above attenuation and bandwidth criteria for all allowable FOIRL lengths, and assuming up to 4 dB of connection losses within the optical fiber cable link segment, it is recommended that the cabled optical fiber have an attenuation $\leq$ 4 dB/km and a bandwidth length product $\geq$ 150 MHz·km at a wavelength of 850 nm.

The total incremental optical pulse edge jitter introduced by the optical fiber cable link segment shall be less than 1 ns when driven by an optical transmitter as specified in 9.9.4.1. The pulse delay introduced by the optical fiber cable shall not exceed 50 bit times for a 1 km length.

Interoperability of FOMAUs using fiber sizes other than the 62.5/125 μm is assured provided that the received peak optical power is between -27 dBm and -9 dBm.

9.9.5.2 Optical Medium Connector Plug and Socket. The two optical fibers contained in the optical fiber cable link segment shall be terminated at each end in an optical connector plug as specified in IEC Publication 874-2 [13].

The corresponding mating connector socket shall conform with the specifications given in IEC Publication 874-2 [13]. This document specifies the mechanical mating face dimensions to ensure mechanical intermatability without physical damage, of all FSMA connectors covered by the document. In addition, the optical insertion loss when interconnecting two optical connector plugs shall not exceed 2.5 dB (measured using a socket adaptor conforming to the mechanical specifications given in IEC Publication 874-2 [13] and also using two identical fibers, as specified in 9.9.5.1, assuming uniform mode distribution launch conditions).

9.9.6 System Requirements

9.9.6.1 Optical Transmission System Considerations. 9.9.4.2.1 specifies that the BER shall be $< 10^{-10}$ for peak optical powers at the output of the FOMAU's receive optical fiber between -27 dBm and -9 dBm. The value of -9 dBm corresponds to the maximum allowable peak optical power that can be coupled into the worst-case optical fiber specified in 9.9.5.1 at the beginning of the FOMAU's lifetime (see 9.9.4.1.8), and assumes zero optical loss between the optical source output and the optical detector input.

The value of -27 dBm is calculated by subtracting the FOIRL flux budget from the minimum allowable peak optical power that can be coupled into the FOMAU's transmit optical fiber at the beginning of the FOMAU's lifetime (see 9.9.4.1.8). The flux budget is the maximum loss that is allowed within the FOIRL to guarantee a BER $< 10^{-10}$ assuming worst-case link components. A portion of the flux budget has been allocated as a design margin to allow for degradation and tolerance effects in the optical source. This is noted in the following table as the optical source lifetime degradation. The remaining flux budget of 9 dB assumes a system margin allowance for the optical fiber cable link segment over its lifetime, and may be allocated to the optical fiber cable link segment loss at the discretion of the network planner/installer. The following summarizes the allocated optical flux budgets for the worst-case optical fiber of dimension 62.5 μm - 3 μm (ie, 59.5 μm) core diameter and 0.275 - 0.015 (ie, 0.260) numerical aperture:

Start of life minimum peak coupled optical power (9.9.4.1.8)	:	-15 dBm
Optical source lifetime degradation	:	3 dB
Maximum optical fiber cable link segment loss including system margin allowance	:	9 dB
Resultant required receive peak optical power	:	-27 dBm

9.9.6.2 Timing Considerations. Table 9-1 summarizes the maximum allowable timing budget contributions to the system timing budget for the FOIRL. The Last Bit In to Last Bit Out delay shall equal the Steady-State Propagation delay.

9.9.7 Environmental Specifications

9.9.7.1 Safety Requirements

9.9.7.1.1 Electrical Safety. A major application for the vendor independent FOIRL is for interconnecting 10BASE5 and/or 10BASE2 coaxial cable segments located within different buildings. The level of isolation provided by the optical fiber cable link segment shall be consistent with this application and provide adequate personnel and equipment safety from earth faults and lightning strike hazards.

Table 9-1
Maximum Allowable Timing Budget Contributions to the FOIRL System Timing Budget

Symbol	Function	Bit Loss (Bit Times)	Invalid Bits (Bit Times)	Steady-State Propagation Delay (Bit Times)	Start-Up Delay (Bit Times)
I1	OPTICAL DATA IN ASSERT→INPUT	2.0	1.0	0.5	3.5
I2	OUTPUT→OPTICAL DATA OUT ASSERT	2.0	1.0	0.5	3.5
LOOP BACK	DO CIRCUIT ASSERT →DI CIRCUIT ASSERT	5.0	1.0	1.0	7.0
I3	OPTICAL COLLISION →SQE ASSERT	—	—	—	3.5
I4	COLLISION DEASSERT →SQE DEASSERT	—	—	—	7.0*
A1	AUI Propagation	—	—	2.57	2.57
F1	Optical Fiber Propagation per Kilometer	—	—	50	50

(*Minimum Start-Up Delay for I4 is 4.5 bit times.)

9.9.7.1.2 Optical Source Safety. The recommendations of IEC Document 76(Central Office)6 [14] shall be adhered to in determining the optical source safety and user warning requirements.

9.9.7.2 Electromagnetic Environment

9.9.7.2.1 Susceptibility Levels. Sources of interference from the environment include electromagnetic fields, electrostatic discharge, and transient voltages between earth connections. Several sources of interference contribute to voltage build-up between the optical fiber cable link segment (either a metallic strength member in the cable; or a metallic optical connector plug or the outermost conducting element of the FOMAU for the case of no metallic strength member) and the earth connection of a DTE.

The physical channel hardware shall meet its specifications when operating in both of the following conditions:

(1) Ambient plane wave field of 2 V/m from 10 kHz through 30 MHz and 5 V/m from 30 MHz through 1 GHz.

NOTE: These are the levels typically found 1 km from radio broadcast stations.

(2) Interference source voltage of 15.8 V peak sine wave of frequency 10 MHz in series with a 50 Ω source resistance applied between the optical fiber cable link segment (either a metallic strength member in the cable; or a metallic optical

connector plug or the outermost conducting element of the FOMAU for the case of no metallic strength member) and the earth connection of a DTE.

NOTE: The optical fiber link segment is capable of withstanding higher levels of electromagnetic interference. The above specifications are the minimum requirements for the environment in which the FOMAU is required to operate.

9.9.7.2.2 Emission Levels. The FOMAU and optical fiber cable link segment shall comply with CISPR Publication 22 [1].

9.9.7.3 Temperature and Humidity. The FOMAU and associated connector/cable systems are expected to operate over a reasonable range of environmental conditions related to temperature, humidity, and physical handling such as shock and vibration. Specific requirements and values for these parameters are beyond the scope of this standard. Manufacturers should indicate in the literature associated with the FOMAU (and on the FOMAU if possible) the operating environment specifications to facilitate selection, installation, and maintenance of these components. It is further recommended that such specifications be stated in standard terms, as specified in IEC Document 68 [15].

ANSI/IEEE
Std 802.3b-1985
(Supplement to ANSI/IEEE Std 802.3-1988)

An American National Standard

Broadband Medium Attachment Unit and Broadband Medium Specifications, Type 10BROAD36 (Section 11)

Sponsor
IEEE Computer Society

Approved September 19, 1985
IEEE Standards Board

Approved February 28, 1986
American National Standards Institute

When the IEEE 802.3 Working Group approved this standard in February 1985, it had the following membership.

Don Loughry, *Chairman*
Menachem Abraham, *Chairman, Type 10BROAD36 Task Force*

Keith Albright
R. V. Balakrishnan
William Belknap
Richard Bennett
Charles Brill
Juan Bulnes
Stephen Cooper
Ronald Crane
John Davidson
Mark Devon
Paul Eastman
Phil Edholm
Gregory Ennis
Judy Estrin
Alan Flatman
Richard Fransen
Ingrid Fromm
Robert Galin
Sharad Gandhi
Rich Graham
Richard Gumpertz
Hacene Hariti
Guy Harkins
Gregory Hopkins
Fred Huang
Stephen Janshego
Donald Johnson
Kwi-Yung Jung
Paul Kellam
Joe Kennedy
Hiroshi Kobayashi
Lee LaBarre
Ed Lare
Tony Lauck
John Laynor
William Livingston
Terry Lockyer
Hugh Logan
Leland Long
James Lucas
Andy Luque
Daniel Maltbie
Joseph Mazor
Steven Moustakas
Narayan Murthy
Wendell Nakamine
Lloyd Oliver
Aidan Paul
David Potter
Eric Rawson
Eugene Reilly
Joseph Rickert
Anthony Rizzolo
Gary Robinson
Timothy Rock
David Roos
Robert Rosenthal
Joseph St. Amand
Walter Schreuer
Semir Sirazi
David Smith
Stephen Soto
Gary Spencer
Robert Summers
Pat Thaler
Geoff Thompson
Nathan Tobol
Wendell Turner
Marc Warshaw
David White
Mo Zonoun

The following persons were on the balloting committee that approved this document for submission to the IEEE Standards Board:

Marshall Abrams
John Adams
William B. Adams
S. R. Ahuja
Kit Athul
William Ayen
Yong-Myung Baeg
Wesley A. Ballenger, Jr
Edwardo W. Bergamini
Henk F. Boley
George S. Carson
Po Chen
L. Y. Cheung
Kilnam Chon
T. Ricky Chow
David Cohen
Allen F. Conrad
Ira W. Cotton
Robert S. Crowder
Michel Diaz
Mitchell G. Duncan
Philip H. Enslow, Jr
Judith Estrin
John W. Fendrich
Harvey A. Freeman
Patrick Gonia
Ambuj Goyal
Michael D. Graebner
Maris Graube
Nobuhiro Hamada
Joseph L. Hammond
Keith W. Harbaugh
S. M. Harris
J. Scott Haugdahl
Sharon Healy
C. W. Hobbs
Jim P. Hong
Paul L. Hutton
Richard Iliff
George D. Jelatis
E. Douglas Jensen
Guy Juanole
Siegel L. Junker
Karl H. Kellermayr
Mladen Kezunovic
Samuel Kho
David Kollm
Sastri L. Kota
Hirayr M. Kudyan
Takahiko Kuki
Lee LaBarre
Wai-Sum Lai
Valerie Lasker
Lanse M. Leach
Edward Y. S. Lee
Stephen E. Levin
F. C. Lim
Don C. Loughry
Joseph F. P. Luhukay
Wo-Shun Luk

Marco Marsan
Joseph Massi
Darrell B. McIndoe
Patrick S. McIntosh
Marco Meli
David S. Millman
Aditya N. Mishra
Richard J. Moff
David E. Morgan
Mike Morganti
Kinji Mori
D. J. Morris
H. T. Mouftah
Dale A. Murray
Ruth Nelson
J. Duane Northcutt
Charles Oestereicher
David Ofsevit
Young Oh
George Parowski
Thomas L. Phinney
Nikitas Pimopoulos
David Potter
John Potvcek
Gary S. Robinson
Marya Repko
Robert Rosenthal
Gian Paolo Rossi
David J. Rypka
S. I. Samoylenko
Norman F. Schneidewind
Oscar Sepulveda
Omri Serlin
D. Sheppard
R. M. Simmons
David W. Sloyer
Stephen Soto
Tom Stack
Carel M. Stillebroer
Fred Strauss
Bart W. Stuck
Tatsuya Suda
Peter Sugar
Efstathios D. Sykas
Daniel T. W. Sze
Ahmed N. Tantaui
Mario Tokoro
H. C. Torng
Donald F. Towsley
Wei-Tek Tsai
M. Tsuchiya
Richard Tung
Stanko Turk
L. David Umbaugh
James Vorhies
Pearl S. C. Wang
Don Weir
Alan J. Weissberger
William J. Wenker
Earl J. Whitaker
Bryan S. Whittle
Michael Willett
Donald Wittman
George R. Wood
Tsong-Ho Wu

When the IEEE Standards Board approved this standard on September 19, 1985, it had the following membership:

John E. May, *Chairman* **John P. Riganati,** *Vice Chairman*
Sava I. Sherr, *Secretary*

James H. Beall
Fletcher J. Buckley
Rene Castenschiold
Edward Chelotti
Edward J. Cohen
Paul G. Cummings
Donald C. Fleckenstein
Jay Forster
Daniel L. Goldberg
Kenneth D. Hendrix
Irvin N. Howell
Jack Kinn
Joseph L. Koepfinger*
Irving Kolodny
R. F. Lawrence
Lawrence V. McCall
Donald T. Michael*
Frank L. Rose
Clifford O. Swanson
J. Richard Weger
W. B. Wilkens
Charles J. Wylie

*Member emeritus

Contents

11. Broadband Medium Attachment Unit and Broadband Medium Specifications, Type 10BROAD36

11.1 Scope

11.1.1 Overview. This standard defines the functional, electrical, and mechanical characteristics of the Broadband Medium Attachment Unit (MAU) and the specific single- and dual-cable broadband media for use with local area networks. The headend frequency translator for single-cable broadband systems is also defined. The relationship of this specification to all of the IEEE Local Area Network standards (IEEE 802) is shown in Fig 11-1.

The purpose of the MAU is to provide a means of attaching devices to a broadband local network medium. The medium comprises CATV-type cable, taps, connectors, and amplifiers. A coaxial broadband system permits the assignment of different frequency bands to multiple applications. For example, a band in the spectrum can be utilized by local area networks while other bands are used by point-to-point or multidrop links, television, or audio signals.

The physical tap is a passive directional device such that the MAU transmission is directed towards the headend location (reverse direction). On a single-cable system the transmission from the MAU is at a carrier frequency f1. A frequency translator (or remodulator) located at the headend up-converts to a carrier frequency f2, which is sent in the forward direction to the taps (receiver inputs). On a dual-cable system the transmit and receive carrier frequencies are identical (both f1) and the MAU connects to the medium via two taps, one on the receive cable and the other on the transmit cable. The transmit and receive cables are connected to each other at the headend location. Figure 11-2 shows broadband single- and dual-cable systems.

The broadband MAU operates by accepting data from the attached Data Termination Equipment (DTE) and transmitting a modulated radio frequency (RF) data signal in a data band on the broadband coaxial cable system. All MAUs attached to the cable system receive and demodulate this RF signal and recover the DTE data. The broadband MAU emulates a baseband MAU except for delay between transmission and reception, which is inherent in the broadband cable system.

A transmitting MAU logically compares the beginning of the received data with the data transmitted. Any difference between them, which may be due to errors caused by colliding transmissions, or reception of an earlier transmission from another MAU, or a bit error on the channel, is interpreted as a collision.

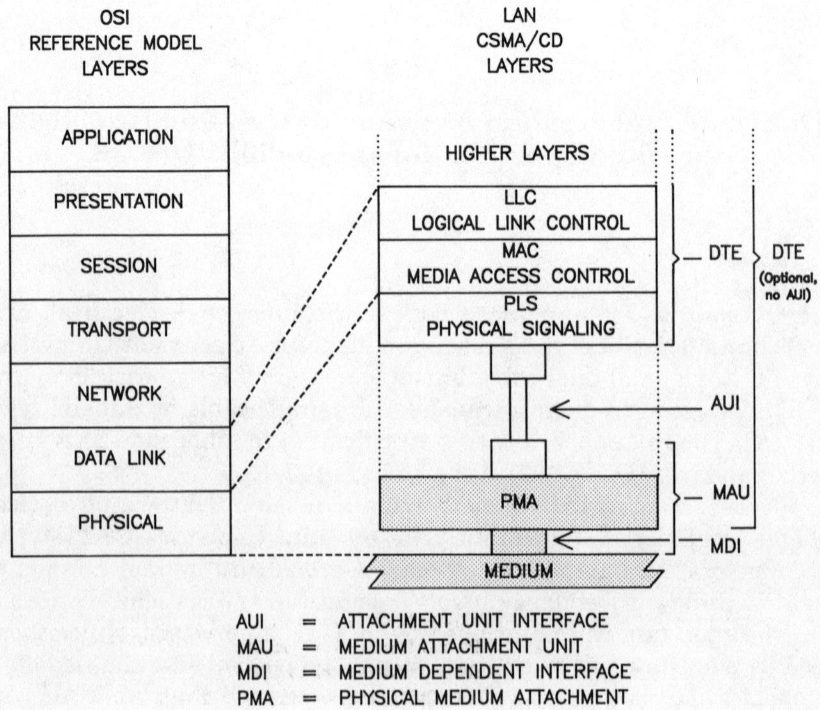

Fig 11-1
Physical Layer Partitioning; Relationship to the ISO Open System Interconnection Reference Model

When a collision is recognized, the MAU stops transmission in the data band and begins transmission of an RF collision enforcement (CE) signal in a separate CE band adjacent to the data band. The CE signal is detected by all MAUs and informs them that a collision has occurred. All MAUs signal to their attached Medium Access Controllers (MACs) the presence of the collision. The transmitting MACs then begin the collision handling process.

Collision enforcement is necessary because RF data signals from different MAUs on the broadband cable system may be received at different power levels. During a collision between RF data signals at different levels, the MAU with the higher received power level may see no errors in the detected data stream. However, the MAU with the lower RF signal will see a difference between transmitted and received data; this MAU transmits the CE signal to force recognition of the collision by all transmitting MAUs.

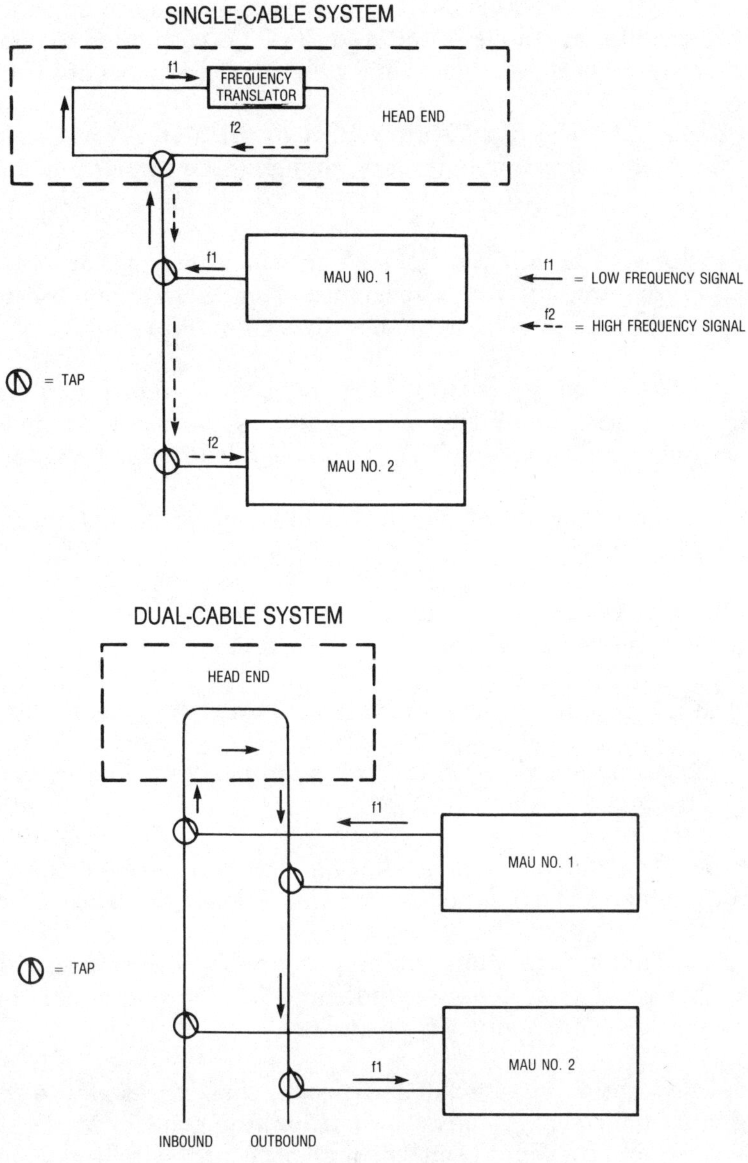

Fig 11-2
Broadband Cable Systems

11.1.2 Definitions

Attachment Unit Interface (AUI). In a local area network, the interface between the medium attachment unit and the DTE within a data station. Note that the AUI carries encoded signals and provides for duplex data transmission.

Binary Phase Shift Keying (Binary PSK or BPSK). A form of modulation in which binary data are transmitted by changing the carrier phase by 180 degrees.

Broadband LAN. A Local Area Network in which information is transmitted on modulated carriers, allowing coexistence of multiple simultaneous services on a single physical medium by frequency division multiplexing.

CATV-Type Broadband Medium. A broadband system comprising coaxial cables, taps, splitters, amplifiers, and connectors the same as those used in Community Antenna Television (CATV) or cable television installations.

Channel. A band of frequencies dedicated to a certain service transmitted on the broadband medium.

Coaxial Cable. A two conductor, concentric (center conductor and shield), constant impedance transmission line.

Continuous Wave (CW). A carrier that is not modulated or switched.

dBmV. Decibels referenced to 1.0 mV on 75 Ω, used to define signal levels in CATV-type broadband systems.

Drop Cable. The small diameter flexible coaxial cable of the broadband medium that connects to a Medium Access Unit (MAU). See **Trunk Cable** .

Group Delay. The rate of change of total phase shift, with respect to frequency, through a component or system. Group delay variation is the maximum difference in group delay over a band of frequencies.

Headend. The location in a broadband system that serves as the root for the branching tree comprising the physical medium; the point to which all inbound signals converge and the point from which all outbound signals emanate.

Jabber. A condition wherein a station transmits for a period of time longer than the maximum permissible packet length, usually due to a fault condition.

Postamble. In the broadband Medium Attachment Unit specified in this section, the bit pattern appended after the last bit of the Frame Check Sequence; the Broadband End-of-Frame Delimiter (BEOFD).

Return Loss. The ratio in decibels of the power reflected from a port to the power incident to the port. An indicator of impedance matching in a broadband system.

Seed. The twenty-three (23) bits residing in the scrambler shift register prior to the transmission of a packet.

Spectrum Mask. A graphic representation of the required power distribution as a function of frequency for a modulated transmission.

Translation. In a single-cable system, the process by which incoming transmissions at one frequency are converted to another frequency for outgoing transmission. The translation takes place at the headend.

Truncation Loss. In a modulated data waveform, the power difference before and after implementing the filtering necessary to constrain its spectrum to a specified frequency band.

Trunk Cable. The main (large-diameter) cable of a broadband coaxial cable system. See **Drop Cable.**

11.1.3 MAU and Medium Objectives. This subsection states the broad objectives and assumptions underlying the specifications defined throughout this section of the standard.

(1) Provide the physical means for communication among local network Data Link Entities using a broadband coaxial medium.

(2) Provide a broadband Medium Attachment Unit (MAU) that is compatible at the Attachment Unit Interface (AUI) with DTEs used on a baseband medium.

(3) Provide a broadband MAU that emulates the baseband MAU except for the signal delay from Circuit DO to Circuit DI.

(4) Provide a broadband MAU that detects collisions within the timing constraints specified in the baseband case.

(5) Provide a broadband network diameter no less than 2800 m.

(6) Provide a broadband Physical Layer that ensures that no MAU is allowed to capture the medium during a collision due to signal level advantage (that is, ensures fairness of the physical layer).

(7) Provide a broadband MAU that detects collisions in both receive and transmit modes.

(8) Provide a broadband MAU that requires a transmission bandwidth no wider than 18 MHz.

(9) Define a physical interface that can be implemented independently among different manufacturers of hardware and achieve the intended level of compatibility when interconnected in a common broadband local area network.

(10) Provide a communication channel capable of high bandwidth and low bit error rate performance. The resultant mean bit error rate at the physical layer service interface should be less than one part in 10^8 (on the order of one part in 10^9 at the link level) in a worst-case signal-to-noise ratio of 26 dB.

(11) Provide a broadband medium physical layer that allows for implementation in both dual and single cable systems.

(12) Provide for ease of installation and service.

(13) Provide a communication channel that coexists with other channels on the same physical medium.

It is not an objective of this broadband MAU to allow its use with the baseband repeater defined in Section 9 of this standard.

11.1.4 Compatibility Considerations. All implementations of the broadband coaxial system shall be compatible at the Medium Dependent Interface (MDI). This standard provides medium specifications for the interconnection of all MAU devices. The medium itself, the functional capability of the MAU and the AU Interface are defined to provide the highest possible level of compatibility among devices designed by different manufacturers. Designers are free to implement circuitry within the MAU in an application-dependent manner provided the MDI and AUI specifications are satisfied. Subsystems based on this specification may be implemented in several different ways provided compatibility at the medium is maintained. It is possible, for example, to design an integrated station where the MAU is contained within a physical DTE system component, thereby eliminating the AUI cable.

11.1.5 Relationship to PLS and AUI. The broadband MAU and cable system specifications are closely related to Section 7 (Physical Signaling and Attachment Unit Interface Specifications). The design of a physical MAU component requires the use of both this section and the PLS and AUI specifications in Section 7.

11.1.6 Mode of Operation. In its normal mode of operation, the MAU functions as a direct connection between the DTE and the broadband medium. Data from the DTE are transmitted onto the broadband coaxial system and all inband data on the coaxial cable system is received by the DTE. This mode is the mode of operation for the intended message traffic between stations. Other operating modes, such as a loopback mode or a monitor mode, may be provided but are not defined by this standard.

11.2 MAU Functional Specifications

11.2.1 MAU Functional Requirements. The MAU component provides the means by which signals on the physically separate AUI signal circuits to and from the DTE and their associated interlayer messages are coupled to the broadband coaxial medium. To achieve this basic objective, the MAU component contains the following capabilities to handle message flow between the DTE and the broadband medium:

(1) Transmit Function. The ability to transmit serial data bit streams originating at the local DTE in a band-limited modulated RF carrier form, to one or more remote DTEs on the same network.

(2) Receive Function. The ability to receive a modulated RF data signal in the band of interest from the broadband coaxial medium and demodulate it into a serial bit stream.

(3) Collision Presence Function. The ability to detect the presence of two or more stations' concurrent transmissions.

(4) Jabber Function. The ability of the MAU itself to interrupt the transmit function and inhibit an abnormally long output data stream.

11.2.1.1 Transmit Function Requirements. The transmit function shall include the following capabilities:

(1) Receive Manchester encoded data sent by the local DTE to the attached MAU on Circuit DO (transmit data pair).

(2) Decode the Manchester encoded data received on Circuit DO to produce NRZ (Non-Return to Zero) data and a recovered clock signal.

(3) Scramble the NRZ data using a CCITT V.29-type scrambler with seed changed on each transmitted packet.

(4) Transform the incoming bits (prior to modulation) to provide an unscrambled alternating zero-one pattern terminated by an Unscrambled Mode Delimiter (UMD); scramble the remainder of the incoming preamble, Start Frame Delimiter (SFD), and data frame; and append an unscrambled postamble (Broadband End of Frame Delimiter [BEOFD]).

(5) Differentially encode the packet generated above.

(6) Produce a bandlimited, double sideband suppressed carrier, binary PSK modulated RF signal representing the above generated differentially encoded packet.

(7) Drive the coaxial cable with the modulated RF signal.

Figure 11-3 functionally represents these capabilities. The order of the functional blocks may be altered provided that the result is the same.

11.2.1.2 Receive Function Requirements. The receive function shall include the following:

(1) Receive the differentially encoded binary PSK modulated RF signal from the broadband coaxial medium.

(2) Receive the data band RF signals and reject signals in bands other than the data band (rejection of signals in the adjacent collision enforcement band is optional).

(3) Demodulate and differentially decode the incoming RF data signal from the coaxial medium to provide a receive bit stream that represents the scrambled bit stream at the transmitter.

(4) Descramble the receive bit stream using a self-synchronizing descrambler.

(5) Manchester encode the descrambled bit stream.

(6) Send to the DTE, using Circuit DI (receive data pair), an additional, locally-generated, Manchester encoded preamble equal to the number of preamble bits lost in the receive data path (plus or minus one bit), followed by the Manchester encoded bit stream. No more than 6 preamble bits may be lost from the preamble presented to Circuit DO at the transmitting MAU.

(7) Detect end of frame, using the postamble (BEOFD), and ensure that no extraneous bits are sent to the DTE on Circuit DI.

(8) Receive signals in the collision enforcement band and reject signals in the data band and all other bands on the broadband medium.

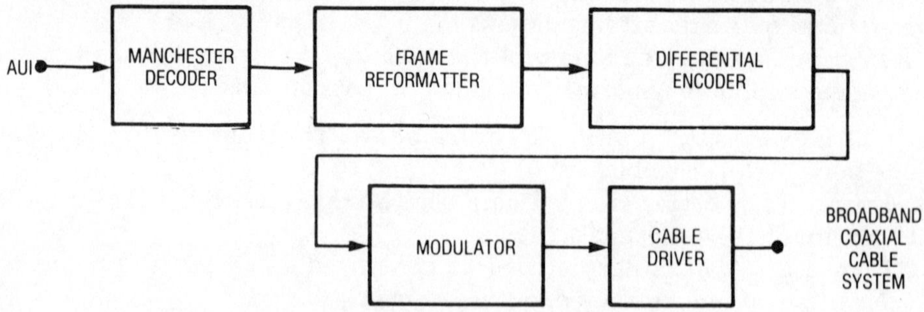

Fig 11-3
Transmit Function Requirements

11.2.1.3 Collision Detection Function Requirements. The MAU shall perform the following functions to meet the collision detection requirements:

(1) Store the scrambled bits (not differentially encoded) in the transmit section through to the last bit in the source address.

(2) Detect the UMD in the transmit and receive paths.

(3) Compare received scrambled bits after the received UMD with transmitted scrambled bits after the transmit UMD through to the last bit in the source address.

(4) A Receive UMD Timer function shall be performed by the MAU. The timer shall be as long as the time required from initial detection of RF data signal presence to detection of a UMD in a normally received (no collision) packet.

(5) Enter a LOCAL COLLISION DETection state if one of the following occurs:

(a) A bit error is found in the bit compare process through the last bit in the source address

(b) The Receive UMD Timer expires before a UMD is detected in the received bit stream

(c) The MAU receives the *output* (that is, transmit) signal from the AUI AFTER having received an RF signal from the coaxial cable

(6) Upon entering the LOCAL COLLISION DET state, cease transmission in the data band and commence transmission in the collision enforcement band for as long as the DTE continues to send data to the MAU.

(7) Upon entering the LOCAL COLLISION DET state send the *signal_quality_error* (SQE) message on Circuit CI (collision presence pair) using the CS0 signal for as long as RF signals are detected on the broadband coaxial medium in either the data or collision enforcement bands.

(8) Detect power in the collision enforcement band and send the SQE message on Circuit CI using the CS0 signal. Send the SQE message for as long as energy is detected in the collision enforcement band.

(9) Ensure that during collisions, due to phase cancellations of the colliding carriers, Circuit DI does not become inactive before Circuit CI becomes active.

(10) Test the collision detection circuitry following every transmission that

does not encounter a collision. This test consists of transmitting a burst of collision enforcement RF signal after the end of the postamble transmission and detecting this burst on the receive side. If the burst is detected, the CS0 (BR) signal is sent on Circuit CI of the transmitting MAU.

11.2.1.3.1 Collision Enforcement Transmitter Requirements. The MAU shall provide a collision enforcement (CE) transmitter that generates a constant amplitude RF signal in the CE band at the same power level as the data signal postamble.

11.2.1.3.2 Collision Enforcement Detection Requirements. The MAU shall detect energy in the CE band that is within the specified range of receive levels, irrespective of the signal power level in the data band.

11.2.1.4 Jabber Function Requirements. The MAU shall have a jabber function that inhibits transmission onto the coaxial cable interface if the MAU attempts to transmit an RF signal longer than 150 ms. The MAU shall provide an MTBF of at least 1 million hours of continuous operation without rendering the transmission medium unusable by other transceivers. Transmissions of less then 20 ms shall not be affected. When the jabber circuit is activated, *signal_quality_error* shall be sent on Circuit CI.

Circuit DO shall also be monitored for transmissions in excess of the maximum packet length. If the packet is longer than 20 ms, an attempt shall be made to deactivate the transmitter before the jabber circuit is activated, to avoid locking up the unit due to a non-MAU failure.

State diagrams defining the jabber function may be found in 11.2.3.

11.2.2 DTE PLS to MAU and MAU to DTE PLS Messages

11.2.2.1 DTE Physical Layer to MAU Physical Layer Messages. The following messages can be sent by the DTE Physical Layer Entities to the MAU Physical Layer Entities (refer to 7.3 of this standard for the definitions of the signals):

Message	Circuit	Signal	Meaning
output	DO	CD1, CD0	Output information
output_idle	DO	IDL	No data to be output

11.2.2.2 MAU Physical Layer to DTE Physical Layer Messages. The following messages can be sent by the MAU Physical Layer Entities to the DTE Physical Layer Entities:

Message	Circuit	Signal	Meaning
input	DI	CD1, CD0	Input information
input_idle	DI	IDL	No input information
mau_available	CI	IDL	MAU is available for output
signal_quality_error	CI	CSO (BR)	Error detected by MAU

11.2.2.2.1 *input* Message. The MAU Physical Layer sends an *input* message to the DTE Physical Layer when the MAU has a bit of data to send to the DTE. The physical realization of the *input* message is a CD0 or CD1 sent by the MAU to the DTE on Circuit DI. The MAU sends CD0 if the input bit is a zero or CD1 if the input bit is a one. The jitter and asymmetry on CD0 and CD1 shall be no more than that specified in 7.5.2.1.

11.2.2.2.2 *input_idle* Message. The MAU Physical Layer sends an *input_idle* message to the DTE Physical Layer when the MAU does not have data to send to the DTE. The physical realization of the *input_idle* message is the IDL signal sent by the MAU to the DTE on Circuit DI.

11.2.2.2.3 *mau_available* Message. The MAU Physical Layer sends *mau_available* message to the DTE Physical Layer when the MAU is available for output. The *mau_available* message is always sent by a MAU that is prepared to output data. The physical realization of the *mau_available* message is an IDL signal sent by the MAU to the DTE on Circuit CI.

11.2.2.2.4 *signal_quality_error* Message. The *signal_quality_error* message shall be implemented in the following fashion:

(1) The *signal_quality_error* (SQE) message shall not be sent by the MAU if no or only one MAU is transmitting a legal length packet (as specified in this standard) on the coaxial medium, except as a part of the SQE self test.

(2) If the MAU connected to the local node is not transmitting, then the local MAU shall send the *signal_quality_error* message in every instance when it detects power in the collision enforcement band earlier than the time equivalent for reception of a 512 bit data frame plus preamble and SFD.

(3) When the local MAU is transmitting on the coaxial medium, all occurrences of one or more additional MAUs transmitting shall cause the *signal_quality_error* message to be sent by the local MAU to the attached DTE.

(4) When the MAU has completed a successful transmission of a packet it shall perform an SQE Test sequence. In this instance, the collision enforcement RF signal is interpreted as an SQE Test signal.

11.2.3 MAU State Diagrams. The operation of the MAU during normal transmission and reception can be described by a state diagram that relates the functions of transmission, reception, collision detection, and collision detection testing. Figure 11-4, at the end of this subsection, shows the state transitions for normal operation. Abnormal conditions are implementation-specific.

The state diagram in Fig 11-4 does not describe the operation of the MAU in detail. This is found in 11.2 and 11.3.

The operation of the jabber function is described by the state diagram of Fig 11-5. When the MAU Jabber state machine is in the INTERRUPT or JAB state, outputs of the MAU Jabber state machine shall override those of the MAU state machine.

11.2.3.1 MAU State Diagram Messages. The following messages are used in the state diagram:

(1) disable_data_driver. Deactivates the mechanism by which the RF data signal is impressed onto the coaxial cable.

(2) enable_data_driver. Activates the mechanism by which the RF data signal is impressed onto the coaxial cable.

(3) disable_CE_driver. Deactivates the mechanism by which collision enforcement RF signals are impressed onto the coaxial cable.

(4) enable_CE_driver. Activates the mechanism by which collision enforcement RF signals are impressed onto the coaxial cable.

(5) *mau_available*. Signifies that the MAU is available for transmission (that is, there is no SQE active).

(6) *signal_quality_error* (SQE). Signifies that the MAU has detected a collision, it has successfully completed the SQE Test sequence, or the jabber circuit is active.

(7) start_SQE_test_timer. Causes a timer to begin counting so that the SQE Test signal may be sent to the coaxial cable interface.

(8) positive_disable. Prevents any RF signal from being sent onto the coaxial cable.

11.2.3.2 MAU State Diagram Signal Names. The signal names used in the state diagram are as follows :

(1) PowerOn. This signal signifies that power has been applied to the unit.

(2) rx_energy. When this signal is active, an RF signal on the coaxial cable has been detected either in the data band or in the collision enforcement band or in both. The delay in asserting or deasserting this signal is sufficiently short that the delays specified in 11.3.4.5 are met.

(3) output. Signifies that data from the DTE is being presented for transmission at the AUI.

(4) tx_umd (Transmit Unscrambled Mode Delimiter). When the Unscrambled Mode Delimiter has been detected in the transmit data sequence, this signal is asserted.

(5) rx_umd (Receive Unscrambled Mode Delimiter). When the Unscrambled Mode Delimiter has been detected in the receive data sequence as it is conveyed from the coaxial cable interface, this signal is asserted.

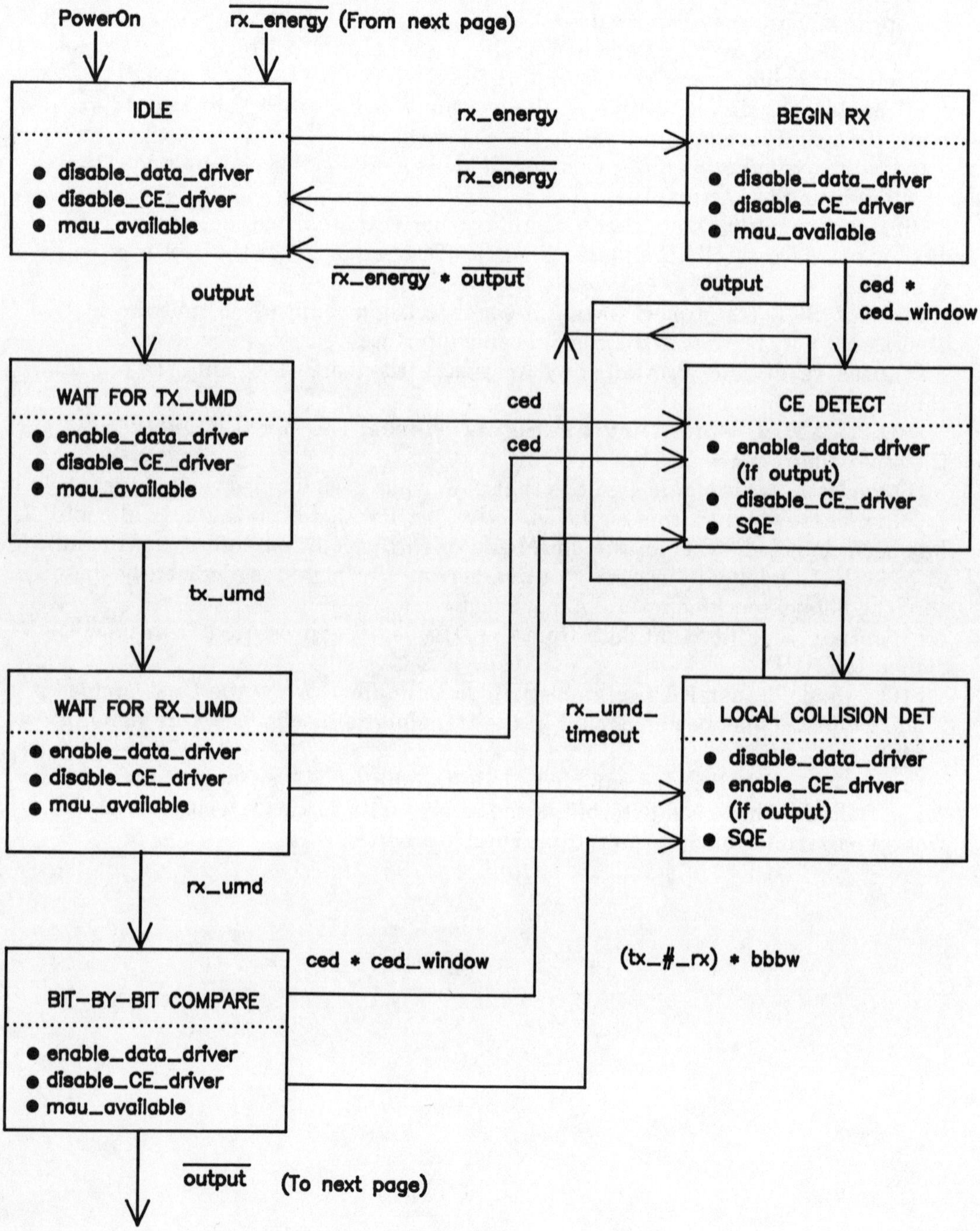

Fig 11-4
MAU State Diagram

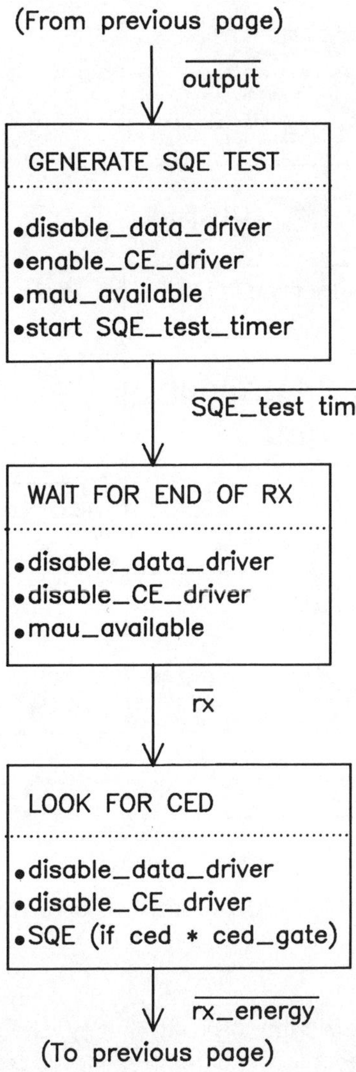

Fig 11-4 ***(continued)***

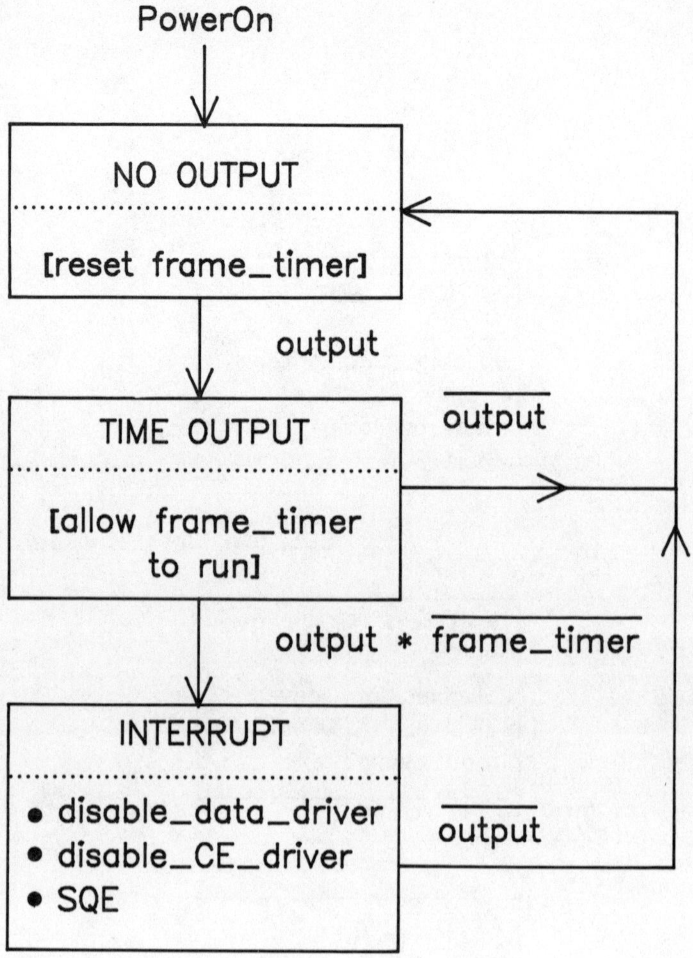

Fig 11-5(a)
MAU Jabber State Diagram

(6) SQE_test_timer. This signal is on during the time that the SQE Test Timer is engaged. At the end of the time, this signal is deasserted.

(7) rx (Receive). As long as data is being presented by the MAU to Circuit DI of the AUI, this signal is active. When the last bit of the receive data has been presented to the AUI, this signal is deasserted.

(8) ced (Collision Enforcement Detection). RF signal power in the collision enforcement band causes this signal to be asserted.

(9) ced_window (Collision Enforcement Detection Window). This signal defines a period of time (a "window") during which collisions may occur. Its purpose is to distinguish collision enforcements from SQE Test sequences on the

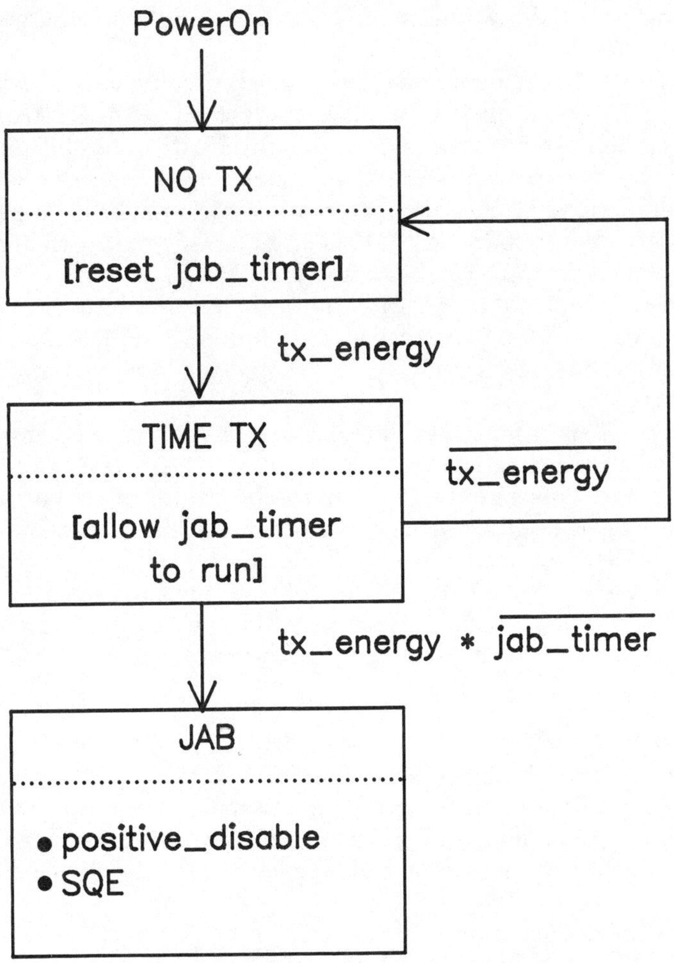

Fig 11-5(b)
MAU Jabber State Diagram *(continued)*

coaxial cable. The window opens when rx_energy goes active and closes a minimum of 365 bit times later. The maximum time the window may be open is the minimum frame length, plus preamble and SFD: 576 bits.

(10) rx_umd_timeout (Receive Unscrambled Mode Delimiter Timeout). It is possible that the Receive Unscrambled Mode Delimiter may be corrupted by a collision such that the bit-by-bit comparison may not begin. This signal forces detection of a collision due to failure to detect the rx_umd within a maximum time. The timeout begins upon receipt of RF signal in the data band and expires 32 bit times later.

(11) tx_#_rx (Transmit Not Equal to Receive). Assertion of this signal occurs

when a difference is detected between the received data stream and the transmitted data stream.

(12) bbbw (Bit-by-Bit Window). Bit-by-bit comparison shall be performed only for a time long enough to guarantee that the last bit of the source address has been examined. This signal is asserted after the UMD is received and throughout the bit-by-bit comparison process. To place a bound on the location of the source address relative to the UMD, the maximum preamble length permitted for operation with the broadband MAU is 62 bits. This places the last bit of the source address no later than 143 bits after the UMD.

(13) ced_gate. This signal is a gating function that serves to shape the timing of ced during an SQE Test. It becomes true a minimum of 6 and a maximum of 16 bit times after the last bit has been presented to Circuit DI and stays active 10 ± 5 bit times.

(14) tx_energy. This signal signifies that the MAU is attempting to transmit an RF signal onto the coaxial cable.

(15) frame_timer. This signal is on from the beginning of output until it is reset or until it has been on continuously for timeout1 s. The value of timeout1 shall be greater than 20 ms and less than timeout2.

(16) jab_timer. This signal turns on when tx_energy turns on and lasts until it is reset or until it has been on continuously for timeout2 s. The value of timeout2 shall be greater than timeout1 and less than 150 ms.

11.3 MAU Characteristics

11.3.1 MAU to Coaxial Cable Interface. The following clauses describe the interface between the MAU and the broadband coaxial medium. The medium is a 75 Ω CATV-type broadband cable installation employing a single bidirectional cable with band-split amplifiers and filters, or dual unidirectional cables with line amplifiers.

11.3.1.1 Receive Interface

11.3.1.1.1 Receive Input Impedance. The nominal input impedance at the receive port shall be 75 Ω. The return loss within the data and collision enforcement frequency bands shall be at least 14 dB with power applied to the MAU.

11.3.1.1.2 Receiver Squelch Requirements. There shall be a receiver squelch that inhibits reception of RF signals that are too low in level. This squelch shall permit reception of RF data or collision enforcement signals that are greater than or equal to -7 dBmV rms as measured by the method of 11.3.1.2.5. RF signals (data, collision enforcement, noise, or other signals) of levels lower than -15 dBmV rms shall be ignored.

The receive squelch for CE signals shall be derived from a power detector with noise bandwidth greater than or equal to 1.5 MHz centered at the CE center frequency.

11.3.1.1.3 Receive Level Requirements. The receiver shall operate with RF data and CE signals having levels from -4 dBmV to +16 dBmV rms. The nominal receive level shall be +6 dBmV rms.

11.3.1.1.4 Receiver Selectivity and Linearity Requirements. The MAU shall operate in the presence of single frequency (CW) signals adjacent to the receive band of the MAU and offset from the band edges, received at the following levels:

(1) 0 dBmV rms at 0.25 MHz below and above the band

(2) 10 dBmV rms at 1.25 MHz below and above the band

The receiver shall be capable of operating in a cable environment loaded with TV signals (for example, every 6 MHz in the USA). The TV signals shall be no higher than +10 dBmV peak video at the receiver coaxial cable interface.

11.3.1.1.5 Receive Input Mechanical Requirements. The receiver mechanical interface shall be a 75 Ω female F-series coaxial connector. The connection to the broadband medium shall be through a coaxial drop cable with a mating male F-series connector. For single-cable configurations, the same connector may be used for receive and transmit.

11.3.1.2 Transmit Interface

11.3.1.2.1 Transmit Output Impedance. The nominal output impedance at the transmit port shall be 75 Ω. The return loss within the data and collision enforcement frequency bands shall be at least 14 dB with power applied.

11.3.1.2.2 Transmitted RF Packet Format. Figure 11-6 shows the transmitted RF packet format.

11.3.1.2.3 Transmit Spectrum and Group Delay Characteristics. The transmit RF data signal shall be binary phase-shift-keyed (PSK) modulated and shall have a frequency spectrum equivalent to baseband raised-cosine Nyquist filtering with a rolloff factor (a) of 0.4, and within the limits of Fig 11-7. For rectangular pulses, the filter characteristic is

$$H\,(jw) = \begin{cases} \dfrac{wT/2}{\sin(wT/2)}; & \left[0 < = w < \dfrac{\pi}{T}(1-a)\right] \\[2ex] \dfrac{wT/2}{\sin(wT/2)} \cos^2\left(\dfrac{T}{4a}\left[w - \dfrac{\pi(1-a)}{T}\right]\right); & \left[\dfrac{\pi}{t}(1-a) < = w < \dfrac{\pi}{T}(1+a)\right] \\[2ex] 0; & \left[w > = \dfrac{\pi}{T}(1+a)\right] \end{cases}$$

where T = one symbol time (100 ns for 10 Mb/s) and a = 0.4, and the first term accounts for the sin x/x spectrum of NRZ random data.

The total variation in group delay from Circuit DO to the RF coaxial medium interface shall not exceed 20 ns in the frequency band from the carrier frequency to ± 5 MHz, and 32 ns to ± 5.5 MHz.

The collision enforcement (CE) signal shall be a constant amplitude pulse with controlled turn-on and turn-off times. Random modulation may be added to reduce the probability of cancellation when more than one CE signal is received simultaneously. The modulated signal shall have an instantaneous frequency within 0.75 MHz of the CE band center frequency and shall conform to the spectrum mask specified in 11.3.1.2.4. The random modulation may be derived from the transmit NRZ data stream.

The CE signal rise and fall times shall approximate a Gaussian shape of the form:

$$f(t) = \exp\left(-\frac{1}{2}\left(\frac{t}{T}\right)^2\right)$$

where T = one symbol time and t < 0 for the rise time and t > 0 for the fall time.

The CE and data RF signals shall not be transmitted simultaneously.

11.3.1.2.4 Transmit Out-of-Band Spectrum. The transmitted power outside the specified band shall meet or exceed the relative attenuation (RA) specified below, under the following conditions:

(1) Transmitted packet length is 256 bits with a 25.6 μs interval between packets, for 50% duty cycle on the cable.

(2) Reference level is an unmodulated carrier, equivalent to the postamble transmitted level.

(3) RA is the attenuation in decibels relative to the reference level outside the specified band, measured in a 30 kHz noise bandwidth with a video filter of 300 Hz bandwidth or less.

(4) B is 18 MHz, the width of data plus collision enforcement bands.

(5) MF is the measurement frequency in MHz.

(6) NCEF is the frequency of the nearest edge of the band, in MHz.

$$RA = \min(63, 55 + 30 \times |(MF\text{-}NCEF)/B|)$$

Figure 11-8 graphically shows the attenuation requirement for out-of-band power.

11.3.1.2.5 Transmit Level Requirements. The transmitter output power during the postamble and during the SQE Test of the collision enforcement signal shall be 1000 mV peak-to-peak into a 75 Ω load (51 dBmV rms). Truncation loss due to the specified data filtering is 1 dB; transmitted RF data

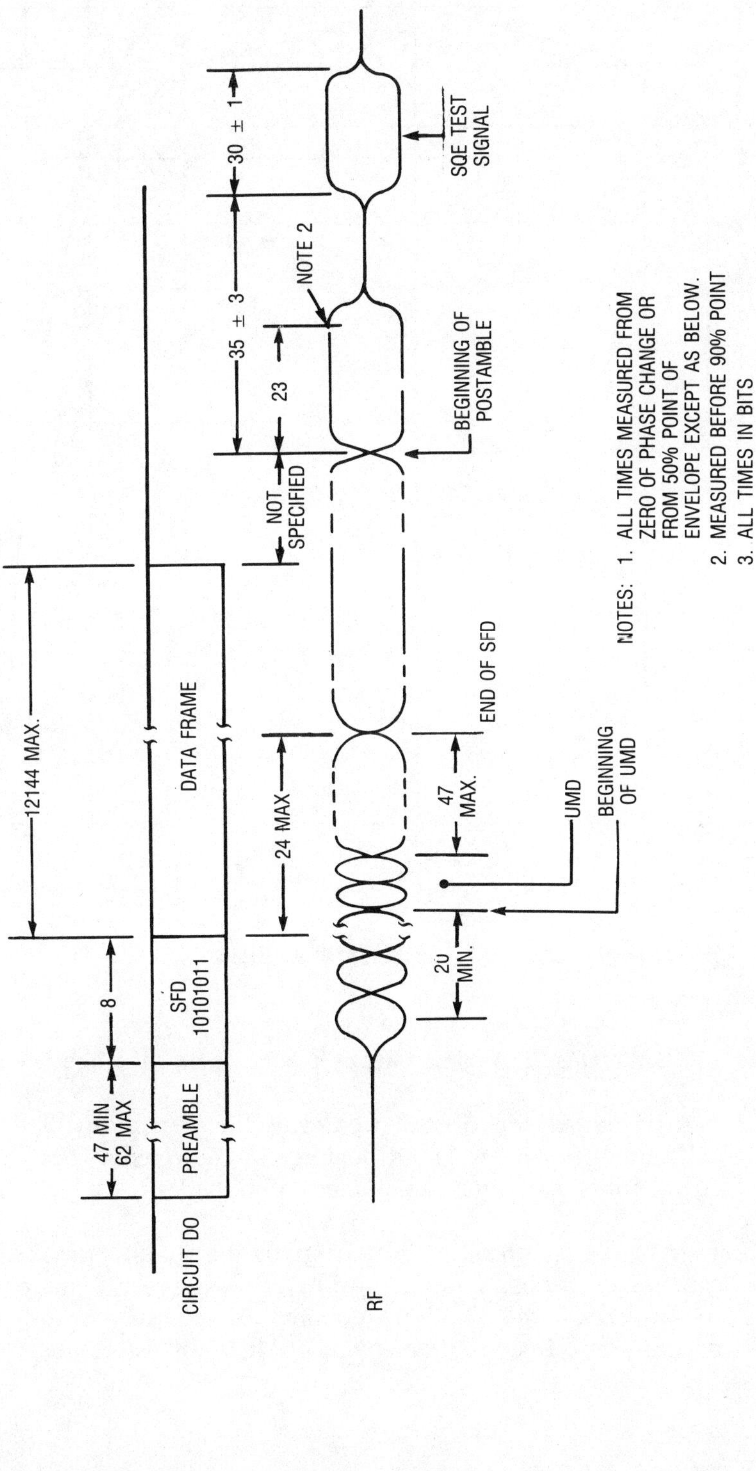

Fig 11-6
Packet Format and Timing Diagram (AUI to Coaxial Cable Interface)

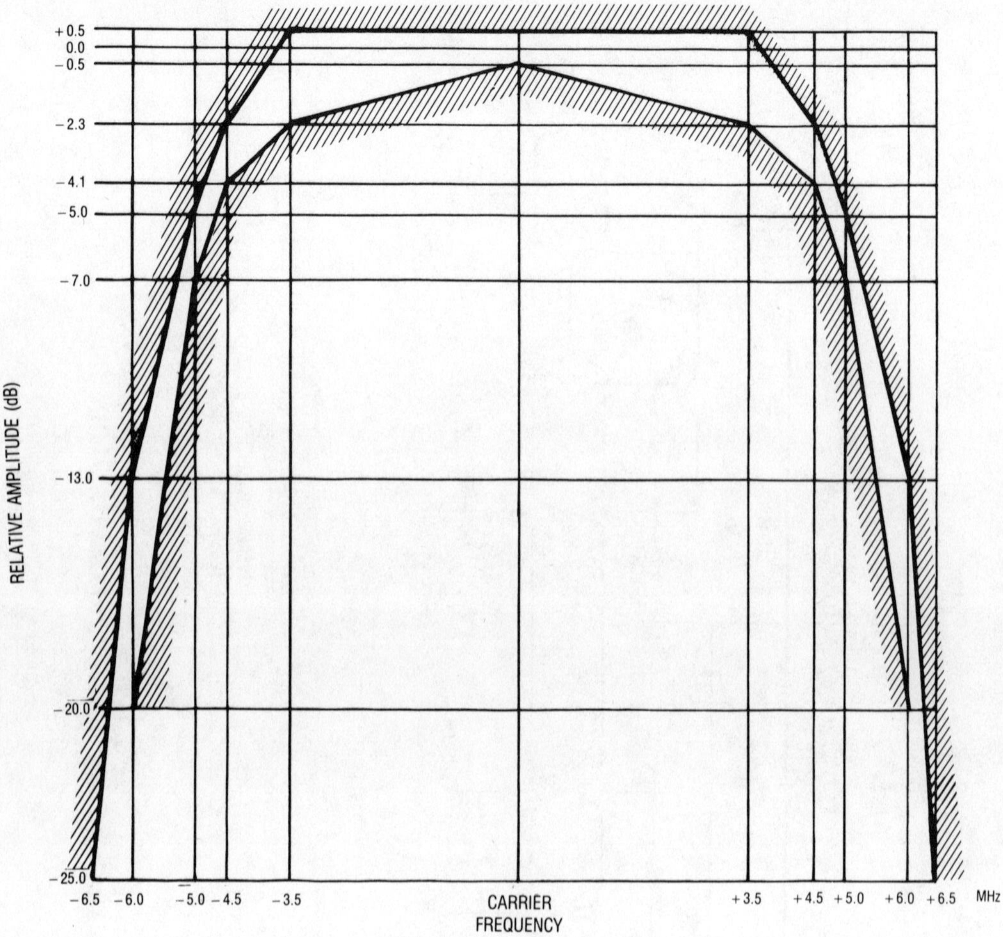

Fig 11-7
Spectrum Mask for RF Data Signal

signal power is 50 dBmV rms. Transmit output power variations shall not exceed ± 2 dB.

11.3.1.2.6 Nontransmitting Signal Leakage Requirement. The RF data signal and collision enforcement signal leakage to the coaxial cable interface while the MAU is not in its transmission mode shall be less than -20 dBmV rms.

11.3.1.2.7 Transmit Spurious Output Requirement. All spurious signals from the transmitter (in-band and out-of-band) while not transmitting shall be less than -20 dBmV rms. All spurious signals from the transmitter while transmitting data or collision enforcement shall be below the spectrum mask specified in 11.3.1.2.4.

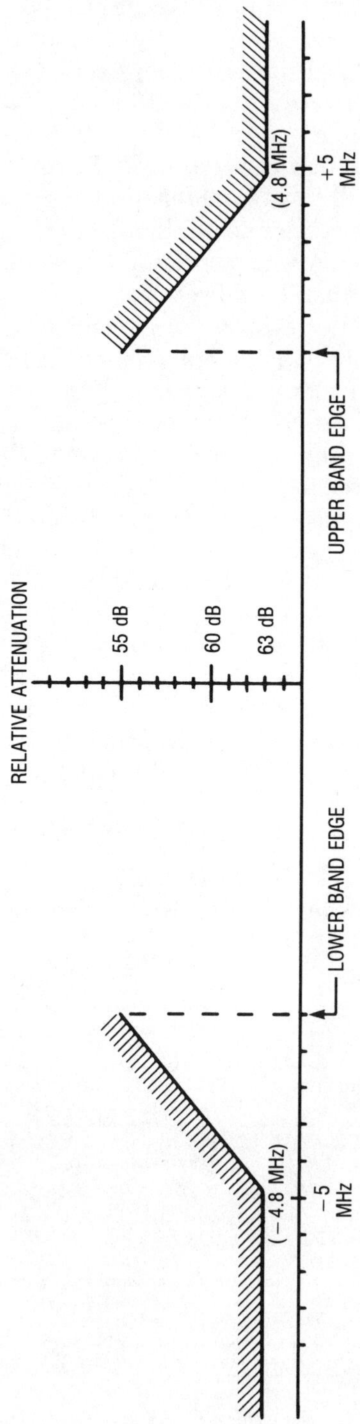

Fig 11-8
Transmit Out-of-Band Power Attenuation

11.3.1.2.8 Collision Enforcement Signal Leakage Requirement. The collision enforcement RF signal leakage to the coaxial cable during data transmission and while the MAU is not enforcing collisions shall be less than 5 dBmV rms. Leakage shall be less than -20 dBmV rms when the MAU is not in the transmission mode.

11.3.1.2.9 Transmit Output Mechanical Requirements. The transmit mechanical interface shall be a 75 Ω female F-series coaxial connector. The connection to the broadband medium shall be through a coaxial drop cable with a mating male F-series connector. For single cable installations, the same connector may be used for transmit and receive.

11.3.2 MAU Frequency Allocations. The broadband MAU uses a data band 14 MHz wide and an adjacent collision enforcement band 4 MHz wide. A single cable midsplit configuration with a frequency offset of 156.25 MHz or 192.25 MHz between forward and reverse channels is recommended. Other configurations, including dual-cable, where forward and reverse channels are on separate unidirectional cables, also are permitted.* The preferred pairing for the usual North American 6 MHz channels is specified in Table 11.2-1 and Table 11.2-2. The tables also specify the data carrier or collision enforcement center frequency for each band, and for single-cable systems, the frequency translation and the headend local oscillator frequency.

11.3.2.1 Single-Cable Systems Frequency Allocations.* Table 11.2-1 lists the permissible frequency band allocations for single-cable systems. The 192.25 MHz translation is recommended for all new designs. The 156.25 MHz translation is allowed for compatibility with some existing systems. The 156.25 MHz translation results in a reversal of the data and collision enforcement bands, as the lower sideband is used.

Table 11.2-1
Single-Cable Frequency Allocations (Frequencies in MHz)

TRANSMITTER			RECEIVER			
			Translation 156.25 MHz		Translation 192.25 MHz	
Data Carrier	Coll Enf Center Freq	Transmit Band	Headend Local Osc	Receive Band	Headend Local Osc	Receive Band
43	52	35.75–53.75	245.75	192–210	192.25	228–246
49	58	41.75–59.75	257.75	198–216	192.25	234–252
55	64	47.75–65.75	269.75	204–222	192.25	240–258
+ 61	70	53.75–71.75	281.75	210–228	192.25	246–264
67	76	59.75–77.75	293.75	216–234	192.25	252–270
73	82	65.75–83.75	305.75	222–240	192.25	258–276

NOTE: (1) Some of these optional bands are overlapping.
(2) Frequency tolerance of the data carrier and headend local oscillator shall each be ± 25 kHz.
(3) + denotes the preferred frequency allocation.

*The remainder of 11.3.2 and all of 11.3.2.1 and 11.3.2.2 are not part of the pending ISO standard. Frequency allocations are a subject for national standardization.

11.3.2.2 Dual-Cable Systems Frequency Allocations.* In nontranslated dual-cable systems transmit and receive frequencies are identical. Table 11.2-2 lists the permissible frequency band allocations. In some instances translated dual-cable systems are installed. In such cases the single-cable frequency allocations may be used.

11.3.3 AUI Electrical Characteristics

11.3.3.1 Electrical Isolation Requirements. The MAU must provide isolation between the AUI cable and the broadband coaxial medium. The isolation impedance shall be greater than 250 kΩ at 60 Hz, measured between any conductor (including shield) of the AU Interface cable and either the center conductor or shield of the coaxial cable. The isolation means provided shall be able to withstand 500 Vac rms for one minute.

The MAU power supply, if provided, shall meet the appropriate national requirements. See Reference [8] for guidance.

11.3.3.2 Current Consumption. The MAU may have its own power supply but is also allowed to use the power supplied by the DTE through the AUI cable. When drawing current from the AUI, the current shall not exceed 0.5 A as provided by the AUI source. The MAU shall be capable of operating from all possible voltage sources as supplied by the DTE through the resistance of all permissible AUI cables. The MAU shall not disrupt the broadband coaxial medium should the DTE power source fall below the minimum operational level under abnormal MAU load conditions. The MAU shall be labeled externally to identify the nominal value of current required by the device at the AUI.

11.3.3.3 Driver and Receiver Requirements. The requirements for AUI cable driver and receiver components within the MAU are identical with those specified in Section 7 of this standard. The drivers shall provide signals that meet the symmetry and jitter requirements of Circuit DI defined in Section 7 and the receivers shall accept signals that have traversed the worst-case lengths of AUI cable.

11.3.3.4 AUI Mechanical Connection. The MAU shall be provided with a 15 pin male connector as specified in detail in the PLS/AUI specifications, in 7.6 of this standard.

11.3.4 MAU Transfer Characteristics. Signals presented on Circuit DO are transformed into signals at the coaxial cable interface by delaying them and by reformatting them. Signals at the coaxial cable interface are transformed into signals on Circuit DI and Circuit CI by a different framing change and by additional delay.

11.3.4.1 AUI to Coaxial Cable Framing Characteristics. Data pre-

*The remainder of 11.3.2 and all of 11.3.2.1 and 11.3.2.2 are not part of the pending ISO standard. Frequency allocations are a subject for national standardization.

Table 11.2-2
Dual-Cable Frequency Allocations (Frequencies in MHz)

Data Carrier	Coll Enf Center Freq	Data Band	Coll Enf Band
43	52	36–50	50–54
49	58	42–56	56–60
55	64	48–62	62–66
+ 61	70	54–68	68–72
67	76	60–74	74–78
73	82	66–80	80–84
235	244	228–242	242–246
241	250	234–248	248–252
247	256	240–254	254–258
+ 253	262	246–260	260–264
259	268	252–266	266–270
265	274	258–272	272–276

NOTE: (1) Some of these optional bands are overlapping.
(2) Frequency tolerance of the data carrier shall be ± 25 kHz.
(3) + denotes the preferred frequency allocations.

sented on Circuit DO shall first be received differentially, then Manchester decoded into an NRZ data stream. The framing of the data shall then be transformed into a new packet for presentation to the RF modulator in the following way (see Fig 11-6 and Fig 11-9):

(1) Up to 5 bits of the incoming data stream may be dropped for detection and Manchester decoding purposes.

(2) Beginning with the first zero, 20 bits of zero-one pattern shall be sent for receiver synchronization and clock recovery.

(3) The next two bits (zero-one in the incoming pattern) shall both be set to zero and form the Unscrambled Mode Delimiter (UMD). The UMD shall take the place of the zero-one in the incoming pattern; it shall not be inserted into the data stream.

(4) All remaining bits in the preamble, SFD, and data fields shall be scrambled (using a CCITT V.29 scrambler plus a differential encoder per 11.3.4.1).

(5) A postamble (BEOFD) consisting of a zero followed by 22 ones shall be added immediately after the last scrambled data bit (the postamble is not scrambled). The postamble may be extended to allow controlled turnoff of the transmitted signal, as shown in Fig 11-6.

(6) All bits (unmodified preamble; UMD; scrambled preamble, SFD, and data; and postamble) are inverted.

(7) All bits sent to the RF modulator are differentially encoded. Figure 11-9

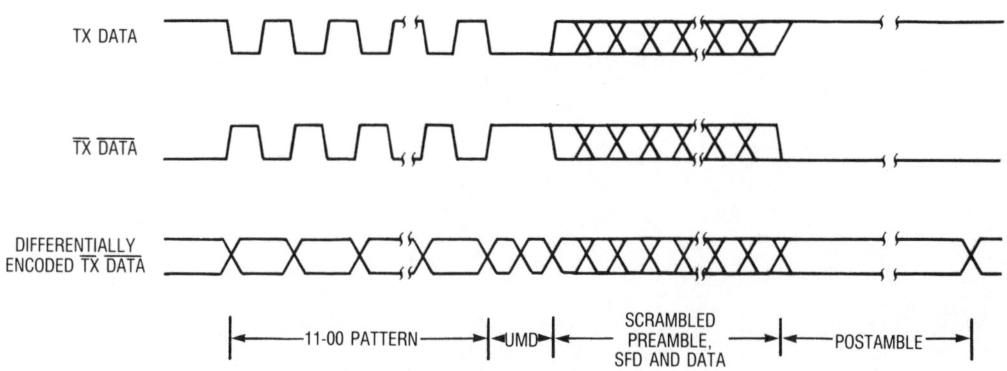

Fig 11-9
Packet Format at Modulator Input

shows the appearance of the data before and after the differential encoder.

(8) The SQE Test sequence shall be generated after a successful data transmission by transmitting a collision enforcement RF signal with the timing shown in Fig 11-6.

Because the preamble of the incoming data on Circuit DO is modified, it is assumed that DTEs generate a minimum length preamble of 47 bits. The maximum preamble length is allowed to be 62 bits, as shown in Fig 11-6.

11.3.4.1.1 Scrambler and Differential Encoding Requirements. The NRZ data shall be scrambled (using a CCITT V.29-type scrambler). A new seed shall be used by the scrambler for every new packet presented by the DTE to the MAU. Figure 11-10 is a diagram of a typical scrambler implementation.

The scrambled NRZ data shall be differentially encoded (see Fig 11-11 for a typical implementation).

The entire encoding process comprising the scrambling and differential encoding is essentially equivalent to a division of the polynomial representing the data to be transmitted by the following polynomial:

$$G(x) = 1 + x^{-1} + x^{-18} + x^{-19} + x^{-23} + x^{-24}$$

11.3.4.2 Coaxial Cable to AUI Framing Characteristics. The MAU shall demodulate, differentially decode, and invert the received RF data signal to recover the scrambled and inverted data stream. Clock shall be recovered and a replica of the unfiltered and noninverted transmitted data stream shall be created. The restored data shall be forced to a logic "one" state whenever no RF data signal is detected. This prevents false UMD detection and forces postamble detection when no carrier is present.

The framing information contained in the RF data stream shall be used to reconstruct the received data so that no more than 6 bits are lost and no more than one bit added to the preamble field, and no bits are added to or lost from the end of the transmit data. Detection of the UMD in the receive data shall ini-

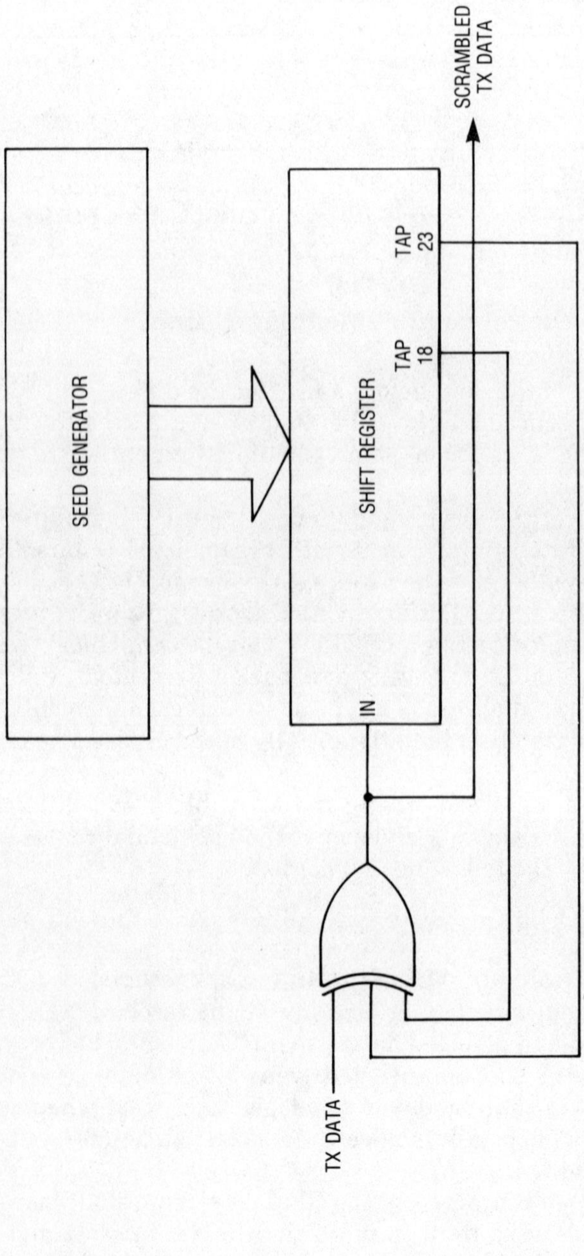

**Fig 11-10
Scrambler**

tiate, after a fixed delay, a locally-generated preamble sequence of zero-one pattern. This pattern "fills in" the preamble bits altered due to the framing information at the beginning of the packet: the zero-one synchronization and clock recovery sequence, the UMD, and the descrambler synchronization sequence.

The MAU shall descramble the received data using a self-synchronizing (CCITT V.29-type) descrambler. No prior knowledge of the seed used by the scrambler shall be assumed by the descrambler circuit. The descrambler shall have valid output no later than 23 bit intervals after the UMD is detected by the receiver. An example of a descrambler is shown in Fig 11-12. The differential decoding performed by the demodulator and the descrambling function are essentially equivalent to multiplying the received polynomial by G(x) as defined in the scrambling and differential encoding requirements subsection above.

After the descrambler is synchronized, 23 bits after the UMD, the correctly descrambled receive data, starting with the 24th bit after the UMD, shall be transferred to the Manchester encoder and therefrom to the AUI. The delay from the detection of the UMD to the beginning of the locally-generated zero-one pattern shall be chosen so that no more than 6 bits of preamble are lost, and no more than one bit added, in transmission from Circuit DO to Circuit DI.

The MAU shall detect the "zero" followed by 22 "ones" (the postamble pattern) and, in conjunction with the loss of carrier detection in the data band or the presence of a collision enforcement detection signal, shall ensure that the packet presented to the local DTE has no extraneous bits added by the MAU to the end of the packet.

The SQE Test signal shall be detected on the RF interface and the SQE signal shall be presented to Circuit CI of the transmitting MAU, subject to the timing restrictions of 11.3.4.5.4. If the signal is not observed at the RF interface due to failure of any element in the transmitter or receiver, no SQE signal may be presented to the AUI. In the event of a collision enforcement, energy will appear in the collision enforcement band within the ced_window time after energy first appears in the data band. Circuit CI shall be asserted when collision enforcement is first detected and shall continue to be active until after the RF signal on the RF port has subsided. Note that an SQE Test signal appended to a packet whose length is less than the ced_window time (less than the minimum allowed packet length) will be indistinguishable from a collision enforcement, except by the MAU transmitting. The transmitting MAU shall take this into account and shall not interpret energy in the collision enforcement band to be a collision when the length of the transmitted packet is less than the ced_window time and the SQE Test sequence has been transmitted. See the discussion in 11.4.2 for more information on ced_window.

11.3.4.3 Circuit DO to Circuit DI Framing Characteristics. In the absence of a collision, the packet format of the receive data at the AUI is identical to that of the transmit data, except that there may be one more preamble bit than was sent at the transmit port and up to 6 bits of the preamble lost. In the presence of a collision, the receive data is undefined, but shall still be properly Manchester encoded.

11.3.4.4 AUI to Coaxial Cable Delay Characteristics. The timing and

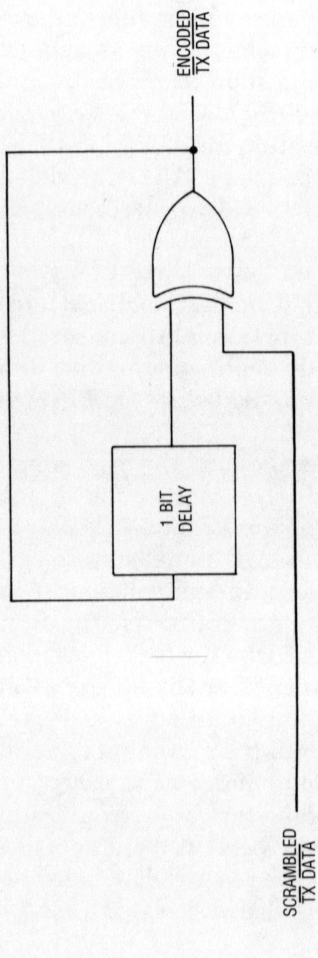

Fig 11-11
Differential Encoder

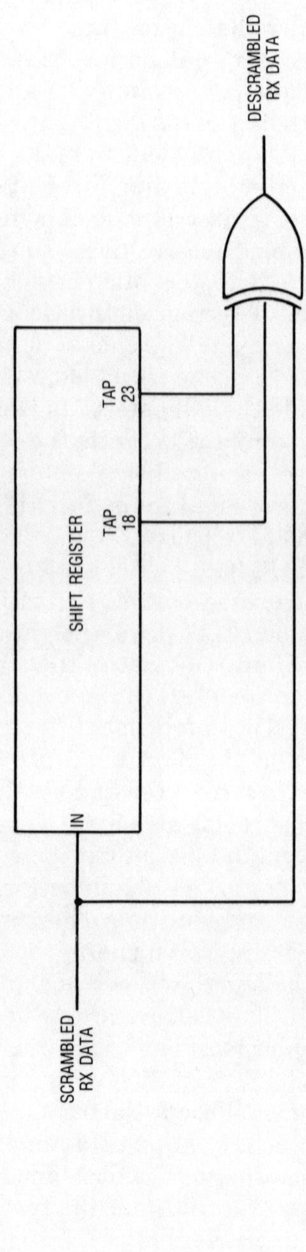

Fig 11-12
Descrambler

delays associated with the transmitter of the MAU are identified below. To ensure compatibility with all MAUs the delays identified below cannot be exceeded nor traded off with other delays in the system.

11.3.4.4.1 Circuit DO to RF Data Signal Delay. The delay from a transition on Circuit DO at the end of a bit to the corresponding phase change of the RF data signal (such bit chosen so that an RF burst phase change does exist) shall be no more than 24 bit times. The delay from the first transition on Circuit DO to the first appearance of RF energy, however, is not specified except as it is determined by other timing constraints.

11.3.4.4.2 Circuit DO to CE RF Output Delay. In the event that the MAU begins receiving energy on the coaxial medium just before the DTE presents data to the AUI, a collision shall be detected locally, as described in Fig 11-4. The delay from the first bit at Circuit DO of the AUI to the presentation of collision enforcement at the coaxial cable interface in this circumstance shall be 32 bit times maximum.

11.3.4.4.3 Transmit Postamble to SQE Test Signal Delay. The delay from the initial transition of the first bit of the postamble (Broadband End of Frame Delimiter) measured at the RF port to the 50% point of the rising edge of the SQE Test signal shall be 35 ± 3 bit times.

11.3.4.4.4 SQE Test Signal Length. The SQE Test signal length shall be 30 ± 1 bit times as measured at the 50% points of the RF signal.

11.3.4.5 Coaxial Cable to AUI Delay Characteristics. The MAU receiver timing and delays described below shall not be exceeded or traded off against any other delays in the system.

11.3.4.5.1 Received RF to Circuit DI Delay. When there is no collision in progress, the delay from the end of the SFD in the received RF data signal at the coaxial cable interface to the end of the SFD on Circuit DI, shall be a maximum of 75 bit times (see Fig 11-13). The minimum is not specified, nor is the delay specified at other locations in the packet. The end of the SFD in the received RF data signal (at the coaxial cable interface) is defined as the time at which the envelope of the carrier would pass through the midpoint if the first bit following the SFD was a zero and the scrambler disabled.

11.3.4.5.2 Received RF to CE RF Output and Circuit CI Delay. In the event that a collision is detected via the bit-by-bit comparison, the delay from the end of the bit in which the collision was detected, as represented by the RF signal, to the 50% point on the rising edge of the collision enforcement signal shall not exceed 34 bit times. The delay from the same point to the first transition of Circuit CI shall not exceed 27 bit times. Circuit CI shall cease activity no more than 31 bit times after activity on the RF interface (in both data channel and collision enforcement channel) ceases. See Fig 11-14 and Fig 11-15.

11.3.4.5.3 Collision Enforcement to Circuit CI Delay. In the event of a collision enforcement by another MAU, the delay from the 50% point on the rising edge of the RF collision enforcement signal to the first transition of Circuit CI shall be no more than 31 bit times. Circuit CI shall be active for a minimum of 5 bit times and shall become inactive within 31 bit times of the cessation of activity on the RF coaxial cable interface, as shown in Fig 11-15.

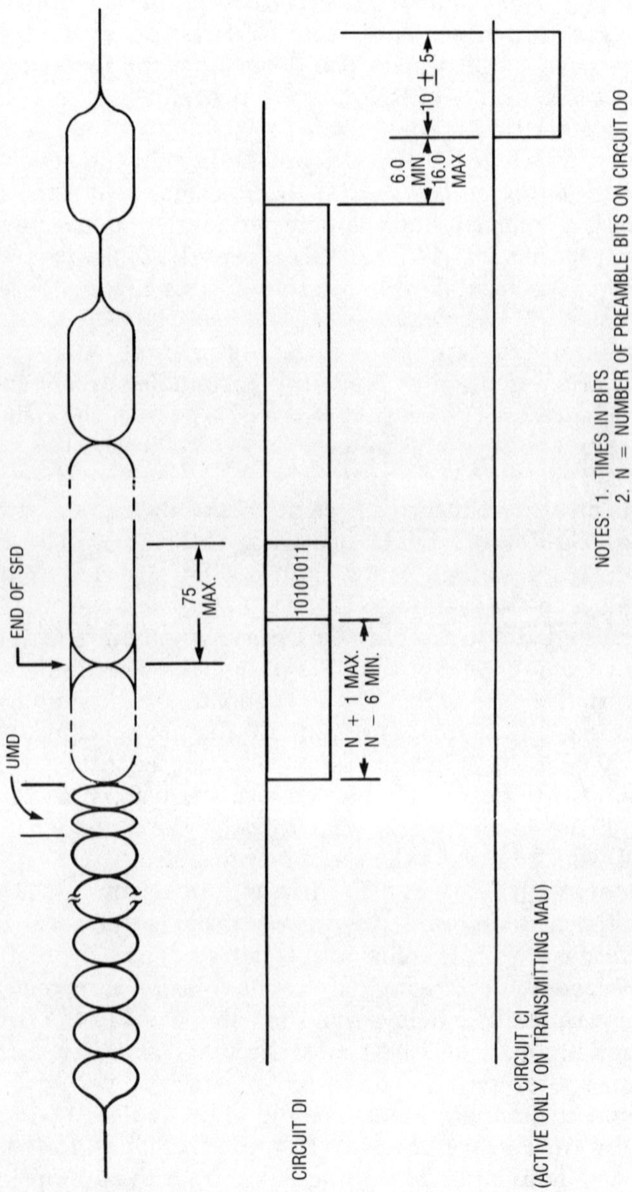

Fig 11-13
No Collision Timing Diagram (Coax to AUI)

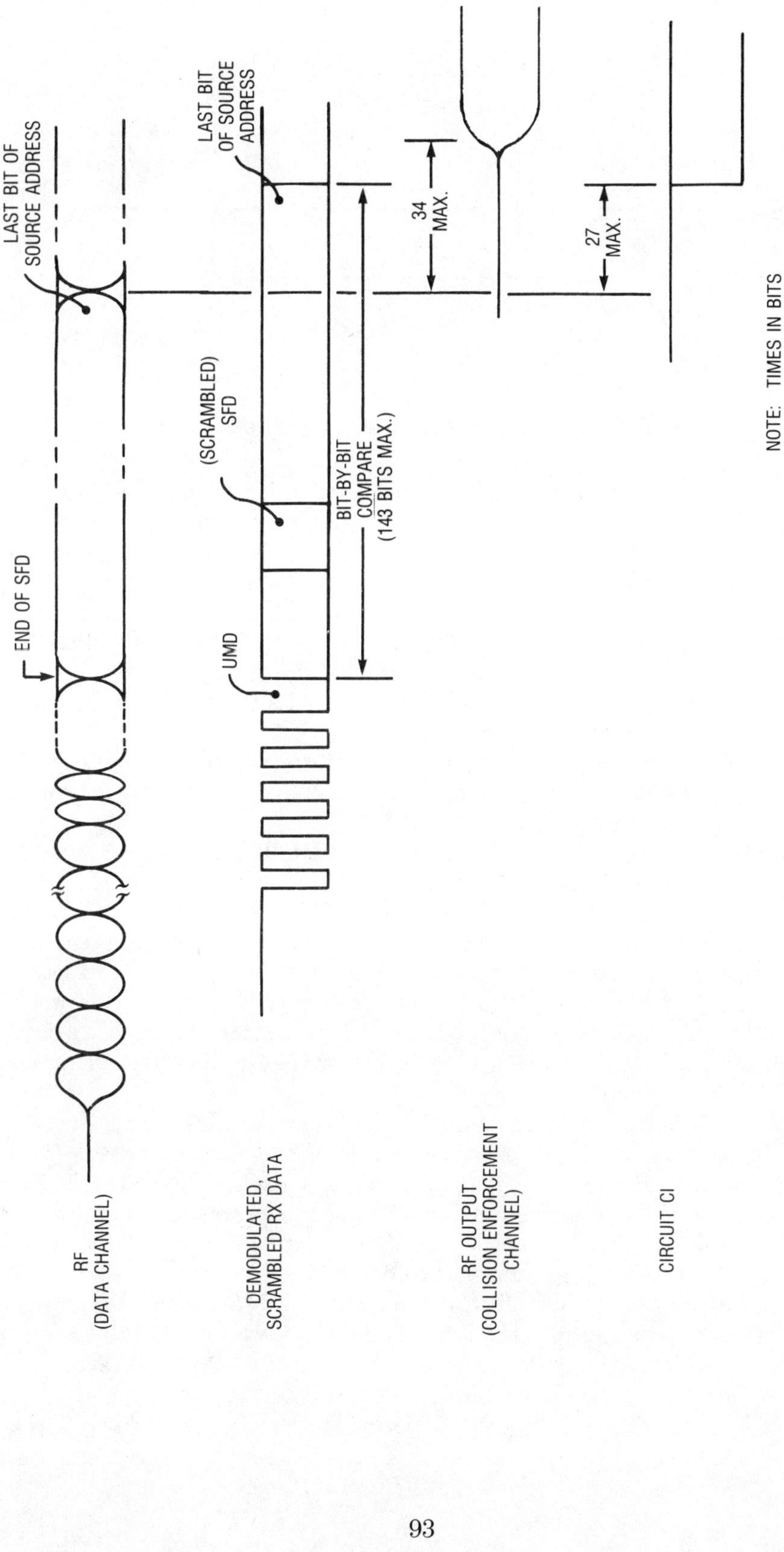

Fig 11-14
Collision Timing Diagram (RF Data to RF Collision Enforcement)

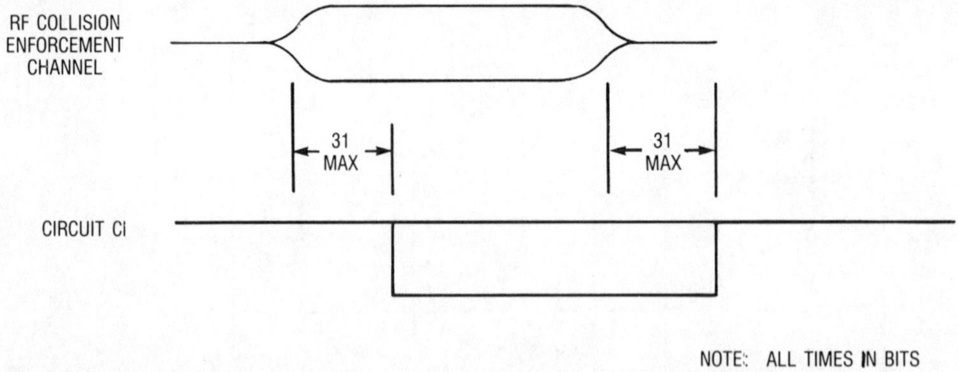

Fig 11-15
Collision Timing Diagram (Coaxial Cable Interface to AUI Circuit CI)

11.3.4.5.4 Receive Data to SQE Test Delay. If a collision enforcement signal is received after the ced_window signal becomes inactive (see (9) in 11.2.3.2), or if the MAU has transmitted an SQE Test sequence, the MAU is to interpret the collision enforcement signal as an SQE Test signal. If the SQE Test sequence is correctly detected (that is, the test passes), then the delay from the last transition of Circuit DI to the first transition of Circuit CI shall be at least 6 but not more than 16 bit times. Circuit CI shall remain active for 10 ± 5 bit times. Only the transmitting MAU shall assert its Circuit CI as a result of successful completion of the SQE Test sequence.

If a collision enforcement signal is received before the ced_window signal becomes inactive, the MAU shall interpret it as a collision enforcement and the timing of 11.3.4.5.3 shall apply.

11.3.4.6 Delay from Circuit DO to Circuit DI. The time delay from a bit on Circuit DO at the AU Interface to the corresponding bit on Circuit DI at the AU Interface is equal to the round trip delay of the MAU connected back-to-back with itself (that is, in RF loopback) plus the round trip delay through the cable system at the location of the MAU. Therefore, the delay is a function of the location of the MAU on the cable system. It is never less than the transmitter delay plus the postamble length plus the time to detect loss of carrier or presence of the SQE Test signal. See Fig 11-16 for the timing relationship when the cable has zero length.

When the MAU is transmitting a short packet (less than 576 bits), the timing for Circuit CI during the SQE Test sequence shall be the same as it is for normal length packets. If the MAU transmits a short packet (less than 576 bits) that encounters a collision and if the SQE Test sequence has not been transmitted when the collision is detected by the MAU, then the timing for Circuit CI shall be the same as it is for any normal collision.

11.3.4.7 Interpacket Gap Requirement. The MAU shall be able and ready to transmit data presented to it by the DTE no later than 90 bit times after the last bit of a received packet was presented by the MAU at its AUI.

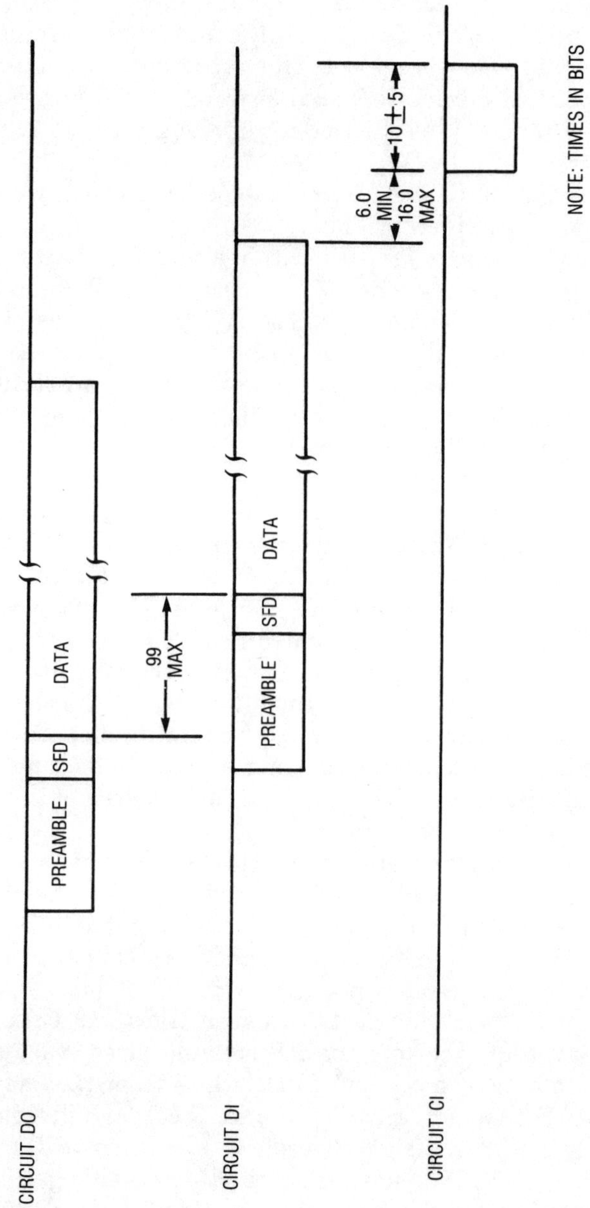

Fig 11-16
Timing at AUI for Zero-Length Coax

11.3.4.8 Bit Error Rate. The MAU shall have a Bit Error Rate (BER) as measured at the AUI lower than one error in 10^8 in a "zero-length coax" test environment (that is, a coaxial cable connection sufficiently short to have negligible delay and transmission impairments). It shall have this BER for receive signal levels in the range specified in 11.3.1.1.3 and in the presence of -28.3 dBmV rms/14 MHz white Gaussian noise. This represents a 24.3 dB signal-to-noise ratio for the specified minimum signal level, -4 dBmV rms. For the same BER in a "system" environment (as opposed to zero-length coax), a 26 dB signal-to-noise ratio is required.

The MAU shall meet the BER requirements specified above when receiving strings of up to 33 consecutive identical bits.

11.3.5 Reliability. Component failures within the MAU electronics should not impede communication among other MAUs on the broadband coaxial cable. Connectors and other passive components comprising the means of connecting the MAU to the coaxial cable shall be designed to minimize the probability of total network failure. The MAU shall be designed to provide an MTBF of at least 1 000 000 hours without causing communication failure among other stations attached to the broadband local network medium.

11.4 System Considerations

11.4.1 Delay Budget and Network Diameter. The delay budget for the broadband MAU and rest of the Physical Layer is tabulated in Table 11.4-1. This table includes allocations for trunk cables (the backbone cables in the system), drop cables (a length of 25 m is assumed), etc. The velocities of propagation assumed are included in the table; use of other types of cables will alter the system diameter accordingly. The types of cables, including the mix of drop and trunk cable lengths, can be altered as long as the total propagation delay from the most distant MAU to the headend does not exceed 70 bit times. The total delay budget of 576 bit times includes allowance for the preamble and SFD (64 bits).

Table 11.4-1 tabulates delay allocations for a dual-cable system with no headend delay. In translated single-cable systems, the headend translator delay reduces the maximum trunk cable distance by [D/(2×CV)], where D is the delay in nanoseconds, and CV is the cable velocity in nanoseconds per meter. For 3.83 ns/m velocity trunk cable, this reduction is [Delay (ns) / 7.66] m.

11.4.2 MAU Operation With Packets Shorter than 512 Bits. The MAU transmits an SQE Test sequence onto the RF medium after every transmitted packet. If the frame plus preamble and SFD is less than the ced_window in length, a receiving MAU cannot distinguish the SQE Test signal from a collision enforcement signal due to a collision. Therefore, operation of the MAU with data frames shorter than 512 bits may cause all other receiving MAUs to see a collision. The transmitting MAU, however, recognizes the SQE Test because that MAU was the one that transmitted the test. An MAU transmitting a short packet that encounters a collision can distinguish the resulting collision enforcement from an SQE Test signal by the fact that the transmitting MAU will not have transmitted the SQE Test sequence unless the packet is shorter than the round trip delay on the cable plant. In the latter instance, the transmitting MAU may not detect a collision enforcement.

11.5 Characteristics of the Coaxial Cable System. The cable system upon which the broadband MAU operates shall meet the following electrical and mechanical requirements.

11.5.1 Electrical Requirements. The electrical requirements of the cable system are listed in Table 11.5-1. Each parameter is applicable over the frequency range to be used by the broadband MAU.

Table 11.4-1
Broadband Dual-Cable Systems—Physical Layer Delay Budget

Delay Element	Maximum Allowed Value (bits)
DTE1 starts to put out first bit	0.00
First bit from DTE1 at AUI	3.00
AUI Cable (50 m at 5.13 ns/m)	2.57
Circuit DO to Tx RF Out	24.00
Tx Drop Cable (25 m at 4.27 ns/m)	1.05
Tx Trunk Cable (1800 m at 3.83 ns/m)	68.95
Rx Trunk Cable (1800 m at 3.83 ns/m)	68.95
Rx Drop Cable (25 m at 4.27 ns/m)	1.05
End of Bit Comparison (last bit of source address)	160.00
Rx RF to Collision Enforcement RF Out (from RX bit that is found to be in error to collision enforcement out)	34.00
Tx Drop Cable (25 m at 4.27 ns/m)	1.05
Tx Trunk Cable (1800 m at 3.83 ns/m)	68.95
Rx Trunk Cable (1800 m at 3.83 ns/m)	68.95
Rx Drop Cable (25 m at 4.27 ns/m)	1.05
Rx Collision Enforcement to Circuit CI	31.00
AUI Cable (50 m at 5.13 ns/m)	2.57
DTE1 Detects Collision Presence	3.00
DTE1 Jams Channel	32.00
Allowance for Taps, Splitters, Amplifiers, and Margin	3.86
Total	576.00

Table 11.5-1
Cable System Electrical Requirements

Impedance	75 Ω
Return Loss	14 dB min
Transmit Level	+50 dBmV ± 2 dB
Receive Level	+6 dBmV ± 10 dB
Maximum Receive Noise Level	−30 dBmV/14 MHz
Loss Variation* (per 18 MHz band)	2 dB max
Path Loss (between any transmit port and receive port, including loss variation)	36 dB min, 52 dB max
Group Delay Variation	
—around data carrier frequency	20 ns/10 MHz max
—over 18 MHz band	34 ns max

*Not including headend.

Adjacent channel signal levels shall be consistent with the requirements of 11.3.1.1.4.

11.5.2 Mechanical Requirements. The connection of the cable system to the broadband MAU is via a standard F-series screw-on male connector. For the dual-cable case, two such connectors are required: one for transmit and the other for receive.

11.5.3 Delay Requirements. The maximum length of the cable system is constrained by the allowable round trip delay from the farthest transmitting MAU to the farthest receiving MAU. Table 11.4-1 allows 140 bit times round trip delay in the cable system. For trunk cable propagation velocity of 3.83 ns/m, this allows 3600 m of trunk cable (round trip; 1800 m from the farthest point to the headend), and 25 m of 4.27 ns/m velocity drop cable at each MAU. In addition, 50 m of AUI cable is allowed on each MAU, therefore allowing, in this case, a maximum of 3750 m DTE to DTE separation. These lengths will be different if cables of different propagation velocity are used. This is acceptable so long as the maximum delay is not exceeded.

For single-cable systems, the maximum delay of 140 bit times includes the delay through the headend. The maximum cable system length must be reduced appropriately, as described in 11.4.1.

11.6 Frequency Translator Requirements for the Single-Cable Version

11.6.1 Electrical Requirements. The headend frequency translator performance is included in the cable system characteristics specified in 11.5, except as defined in Table 11.6-1 below.

The frequency translator contributes to total cable system delay and shall be labeled by the vendor with the input-to-output delay in the band of operation. The effect on network length can then be computed per 11.4.1.

Table 11.6-1
Frequency Translator Requirements

Group Delay Variation —around data carrier frequency —between data carrier and CE center frequency	 20 ns/10 MHz max 50 ns max
Amplitude Variation (from 6 MHz below the input data carrier frequency to 1 MHz above the CE center frequency)	2 dB max
Translation Frequency	per Table 11.3-1

11.6.2 Mechanical Requirements. The input and output mechanical interface shall be 75 Ω female F-series coaxial connectors. The connection to the broadband medium shall be through a coaxial cable with a mating male F-series connector.

11.7 Environmental Specifications

11.7.1 Safety Requirements. This clause sets forth a number of recommendations and guidelines related to safety concerns. This list is neither complete nor does it address all possible safety issues. The designer is urged to consult the relevant local, national, and international safety regulations to assure compliance with the appropriate standards.

Local area network cable systems, as described in this section, are subject to at least four direct electrical safety hazards during their use, and designers of connecting equipment should be aware of these hazards. The hazards are as follows:

(1) Direct contact between local network components and power or lighting circuits

(2) Static charge buildup on local network cables and components

(3) High-energy transients coupled onto the local network cabling system

(4) Potential differences betweeen safety grounds to which various network components are connected

These electrical safety hazards, to which all similar cabling systems are subject, should be alleviated for a local network to perform properly. In addition to provisions for properly handling these faults in an operational system, special measures shall be taken to ensure that the intended safety features are not negated when attaching or detaching equipment from the local area network medium of an existing network.

Sound installation practice, as defined in applicable national and local codes and regulations, shall be followed in every instance in which such practice is applicable.

11.7.2 Electromagnetic Environment

11.7.2.1 Susceptibility Levels. Sources of interference from the environment include electromagnetic fields, electrostatic discharge, transient voltages between earth connections, etc.

The physical MAU hardware shall meet its specifications when operating in an ambient plane wave field of:

(1) 2 V/m from 10 kHz through 30 MHz

(2) 5 V/m from 30 MHz through 1 GHz

MAUs meeting this section should provide adequate RF ground return to satisfy the EMC specification.

11.7.2.2 Emission Levels. The physical MAU hardware shall comply with the applicable national and local regulations for emission levels.

11.7.3 Temperature and Humidity. The MAU and associated cable system are expected to operate over a reasonable range of environmental conditions related to temperature, humidity, and physical handling such as shock and vibration. Specific requirements and values for these parameters are considered to be beyond the scope of this standard.

ANSI/IEEE
Std 802.3e-1987
(Supplement to ANSI/IEEE Std 802.3-1988)

An American National Standard

Physical Signaling, Medium Attachment, and Baseband Medium Specifications Type 1BASE5 (Section 12)

Sponsor
IEEE Computer Society

Approved June 11, 1987
IEEE Standards Board

Approved December 15, 1987
American National Standards Institute

When the IEEE 802.3 Working Group approved this standard in November 1986, it had the following membership.

Don Loughry, *Chairman*

Robert Galin, *Chairman, Type 1BASE5 Task Force*

Menachem Abraham
Keith Albright
Keith Amundsen
Jean-Pierre Astorg
R. V. Balakrishnan
Ian Barker
Charles Brill
Juan Bulnes
Robert Campbell
Luigi Canavese
Albert Claessen
Michael Coden
Bill Cronin
Peter Dawe
Peter Desaulniers
Raymond Duley
Jeff Ebeling
Gianfranco Enrico
Alan Flatman
Richard Fransen
Mark Gerhold
Adi Golbert
Rich Graham
Richard Gumpertz
Hacene Hariti
Lloyd Hasley
Haw Ming Haung
Charles Hoffner
Michael Hughes
Donald Johnson
Mize Johnson
Kwi-Yung Jung
Matt Kaltenbach
Paul Kellam
Scott Kesler
Hiroshi Kobayashi
Hidetsune Kurokawa
Michael Lee
Lee LaBarre
Terry Lockyer
James Lucas
Andy Luque
Luciano Marchitto
Steven Moustakas
Lloyd Oliver
Roy Pierce
Bill Poston
Eric Rawson
Joseph Rickert
Gary Robinson
Timothy Rock
David Roos
Ed Sakaguchi
Walter Schreuer
Semir Sirazi
David Smith
Peter Tarrant
Mark Taylor
Nathan Tobol
Robert Summers
Pat Thaler
Geoff Thompson
Carlos Tomaszewski
Jayshree Ullal
Joseph Wiencko
Bruce Williams

The following persons were on the balloting committee that approved this document for submission to the IEEE Standards Board:

Marshall D. Abrams
William B. Adams
S. R. Ahuja
P. D. Amer
Kit Athul
William Ayen
Eduardo W. Bergamini
H. F. Boley
Paul W. Campbell, Jr
George S. Carson
Po Chen
L. Y. Cheung
Kilnam Chon
W. F. Chow
Michael Coden
A. F. Conrad
Ira Cotton
D. E. Crotty
Robert S. Crowder
Michel Diaz
N. I. Dimopoulos
M. G. Duncan
P. M. Elliot
Philip H. Enslow, Jr
Judith Estrin
John W. Fendrich
G. A. Foggiato
Harvey A. Freeman
Robert J. Gagliano
T. F. Gannon III
Patrick S. Gonia
R. L. Gordon
A. Goyal
M. D. Graebner
Maris Graube
Joseph L. Hammond
Stephen Harris
J. Scott Haugdahl
C. W. Hobbs
Paul Hutton
Richard Iliff
E. D. Jenson
Guy Juanole
S. L. Junker
Karl H. Kellermayr
M. Kezunovic
Samuel Kho
S. E. Kille
David Kollm
Takahiko Kuki
Lee LaBarre
Wai-Sum Lai
Lanse M. Leach
Edward Y. Lee
S. E. Levin
R. C. Lightburn
F. C. Lim
William D. Livingston
Don C. Loughry
Joseph F. P. Luhukay

Wo-Shun Luk
Marco Ajmone Marsan
Joseph Massi
Marco Meli
Darrel B. McIndoe
P. S. McIntosh
David S. Millman
Aditya N. Mishra
David E. Morgan
Mike Morganti
Kanji Mori
David Morris
H. H. T. Mouftah
Dale N. Murray
R. R. Nelson
J. D. Northcut
Charles Oestereicher
Young Oh
George Parowski
Thomas L. Phinney
David Potter
J. M. Potucek
Marya Repko
Gary S. Robinson
Robert Rosenthal
Gian Paolo Rossi
David J. Rypka
S. I. Samaylenko
Norman F. Schneidewind
Omri Serlin
D. Sheppard
Ron Simmons
J. B. Sinclair
L. Sintonen
Stephen H. Soto
Tom Stack
Carel M. Stillebroer
Fred Strauss
Bart W. Stuck
Tatsuya Suda
P. Sugar
Efstathios D. Sykas
Daniel T. W. Sze
Ahmed N. Tantawi
H. C. Torng
D. F. Towsley
Wei-Tek Tsai
Masahiro Tsuchiya
Stanko Turk
L. David Umbaugh
J. T. Vorhies
Pearl S. C. Wang
Don Weir
Alan J. Weissburger
W. J. Wenker
Earl J. Whitaker
Bryan Whittle
Michael Willett
David C. Wood
Tsong-Hu Wu
Oren Yuen

When the IEEE Standards Board approved this standard on June 11, 1987, it had the following membership:

Donald C. Fleckenstein, *Chairman* **Marco W. Migliaro,** *Vice Chairman*
Andrew G. Salem, *Secretary*

James H. Beall
Dennis Bodson
Marshall L. Cain
James M. Daly
Stephen R. Dillon
Eugene P. Fogarty
Jay Forster
Kenneth D. Hendrix
Irvin N. Howell
Leslie R. Kerr
Jack Kinn
Irving Kolodny
Joseph L. Koepfinger*
Edward Lohse
John May
Lawrence V. McCall
L. Bruce McClung
Donald T. Michael*
L. John Rankine
John P. Riganati
Gary S. Robinson
Frank L. Rose
Robert E. Rountree
Sava I. Sherr*
William R. Tackaberry
William B. Wilkens
Helen M. Wood

* Member emeritus

Contents

FIGURES

FIGURES PAGE

12. Physical Signaling, Medium Attachment, and Baseband Medium Specifications, Type 1BASE5

12.1 Introduction

12.1.1 Overview. 1BASE5 is a 1 Mb/s CSMA/CD network based on twisted pair wiring. Each DTE (Data Terminal Equipment) is star-connected to a shared hub through two pairs that function as transmit and receive channels. Hubs can be cascaded, and DTEs can be connected to any hub. Packets transmitted by a DTE are propagated by the hub to a higher-level hub if one exists; otherwise the hub broadcasts the packet back down to all DTEs and lower-level hubs. Packets received by a hub from a higher-level hub are retransmitted to all attached DTEs and lower-level hubs. If two or more DTEs or lower-level hubs transmit concurrently, the hub generates a collision-presence signal that the DTEs detect as a collision. Hubs between a transmitting DTE and the header (highest level) hub propagate data or the collision-presence signal to the header hub; this hub in turn broadcasts the packet or collision signal to all DTEs and lower-level hubs.

12.1.2 Scope. The 1BASE5 specification builds upon the first six major sections of this standard; the remaining major sections (other than this one, of course) do not apply to 1BASE5. That is, the Media Access Control (MAC) and Physical Signaling (PLS) Service Specifications are used in common with the other implementations of this standard, but the Physical Medium Attachment (PMA) sublayer, transmission medium, and hub functions for Type 1BASE5 are specified in this section. The relationship of the 1BASE5 specification to the OSI Reference Model and the IEEE 802.3 CSMA/CD LAN Model is shown in Fig 12-1.

12.1.3 Definitions

bit cell. The time interval used for the transmission of a single data (CD0 or CD1) or control (CVH or CVL) symbol.

bit rate (BR). The rate of data throughput on the medium (in b/s or Hz, whichever is more appropriate to the context). See 12.3.2.4.1.

bit time (BT). The duration (of transmission) of one bit symbol (bit cell) (1/BR). See 12.3.2.4.1.

carrier sense. In a local area network, an ongoing activity of a data station to detect whether another station is transmitting. Note that the signal provided by

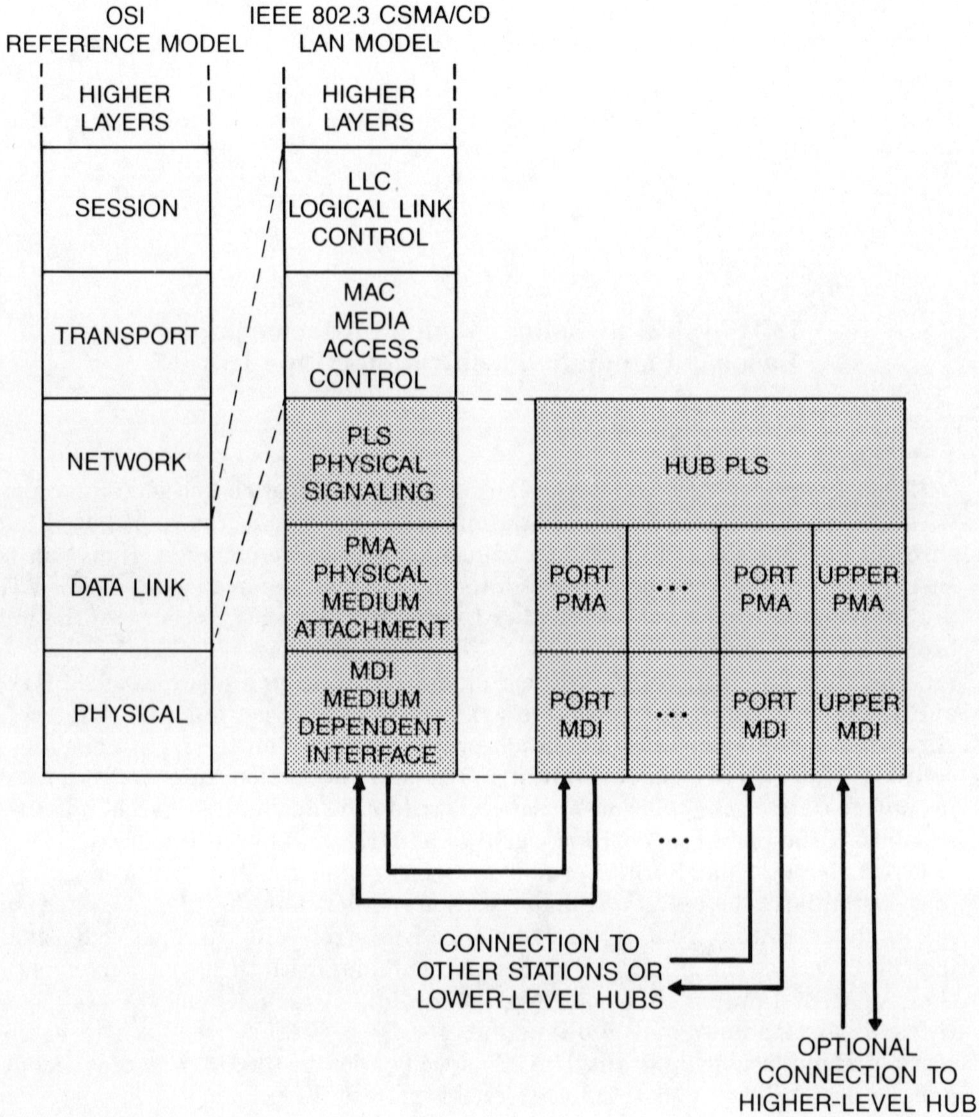

Fig 12-1
1BASE5 Relationship to the OSI Reference Model and the IEEE 802.3 CSMA/CD LAN Model

the PLS to the PMA sublayer indicates that one or more DTEs are currently transmitting.

Clocked Data One (CD1). A Manchester encoded data "1." A CD1 is encoded as a LO for the first half of the bit cell and a HI for the second half of the bit cell.

Clocked Data Zero (CD0). A Manchester encoded data "0." A CD0 is encoded as a HI for the first half of the bit cell and a LO for the second half of the bit cell.

Clocked Violation HI (CVH). A symbol that deliberately violates Manchester encoding rules, used as part of the Collision Presence signal. A CVH is encoded as a transition from LO to HI at the beginning of the bit cell, HI for the entire bit cell, and a transition from HI to LO at the end of the bit cell.

Clocked Violation LO (CVL). A symbol that deliberately violates Manchester encoding rules, used as part of the Collision Presence signal. A CVL is encoded as a transition from HI to LO at the beginning of the bit cell, LO for the entire bit cell, and a transition from LO to HI at the end of the bit cell.

collision. A condition that results from concurrent transmissions on the physical medium.

Collision Presence (CP). The non-Manchester signal generated by hubs to report collisions and some error conditions. See 12.3.2.4.3 for details.

header hub (HH). The highest-level hub in a hierarchy of hubs. The HH broadcasts signals transmitted to it by lower-level hubs or DTEs, such that they can be received by all DTEs that may be connected to it, either directly or through intermediate hubs. See 12.2.1 for details.

hub. A device used to provide connectivity between DTEs. Hubs perform the basic functions of restoring signal amplitude and timing, collision detection and notification, and signal broadcast to lower-level hubs and DTEs.

idle (IDL). A signal condition where no transition occurs on the transmission line. It is used to define the time between packets. See 12.3.2.4.4 for details.

intermediate hub (IH). A hub that occupies any level below the header hub in a hierarchy of hubs. See 12.2.1 for details.

Jabber Function. A mechanism for controlling abnormally long transmissions.

special link (SL). A transmission system that replaces the normal medium. See 12.8 for details.

12.1.4 General Characteristics. Type 1BASE5 has the following general characteristics:

(1) 1 Mb/s signaling rate, Manchester encoded

(2) Twisted pair wiring

(3) Point-to-point interconnection of DTEs to hubs, with one twisted pair serving as the upward link, the other as the downward link

(4) Data pairs can coexist in the same telephone cable bundles as voice pairs

(5) When a hub receives signals from a DTE or lower-level hub, it propagates

them to a higher-level hub if one exists; otherwise, the hub broadcasts the signals back down to the DTEs and lower-level hubs

(6) When a hub receives signals concurrently from two or more DTEs or lower-level hubs, it generates a unique collision presence signal, and distributes it as in (5) above

(7) DTE-to-hub and hub-to-hub interfaces are electrically isolated at both ends

(8) Up to five hub levels are allowed

(9) Hubs serve as repeaters

(10) Maximum DTE-to-hub and hub-to-hub distance is approximately 250 m for telephone wiring (cable-type dependent; see 12.7)

(11) Special links may be used to extend some DTE-to-hub or hub-to-hub distances to 4 km

12.1.5 Compatibility. This specification calls out one principal compatibility interface, namely PMA-to-Medium. It is intended that different implementations of DTEs and hubs be able to interoperate in 1BASE5 networks.

12.1.6 Objectives of Type 1BASE5 Specification

(1) Provide for low-cost networks, as related to both equipment and cabling

(2) Make it possible to use telephone-type building wiring, and in particular spare wiring when available

(3) Provide for easy installability, reconfigurability, and service

(4) Ensure interconnectability of independently developed DTEs and hubs

(5) Ensure fairness of DTE access

(6) Provide a communication channel with a resultant mean bit error rate, at the physical layer service interface, of less than one part in 10^8 (on the order of one part in 10^9 at the link level)

12.2 Architecture

12.2.1 Major Concepts. Type 1BASE5 is a 1 Mb/s CSMA/CD network. DTEs are connected to hubs (and hubs to other hubs) by point-to-point wiring, resulting in a star topology network. Data transmissions are Manchester encoded.

An elementary configuration is illustrated in Fig 12-2. In this instance, each DTE is connected to the hub via separate transmit and receive channels (normally two twisted pairs). The hub serves as the point of concentration and performs two major functions: signal regeneration/retiming (repeating) and collision detection. When only one DTE transmits, the hub repeats the signals, compensating for amplitude and phase distortion, and broadcasts to all DTEs. When a hub detects two or more DTEs transmitting concurrently, the hub generates a unique Collision Presence (CP) signal, which it broadcasts instead of the originally transmitted signals. The hub continues to send CP until it receives IDL from all lower-level DTEs. CP has the property that it can be detected by DTEs as a Manchester code violation.

The interconnection architecture does not imply any minimum, typical, or maximum number of DTEs to be connected to a given hub; this is an implementation or installation detail.

Up to five levels of hubs may be cascaded. A two-level configuration is illustrated in Fig 12-3, with a header hub (HH) and intermediate hubs (IH). There can be a number of IHs; there must be one and only one HH. Each DTE or IH is connected to

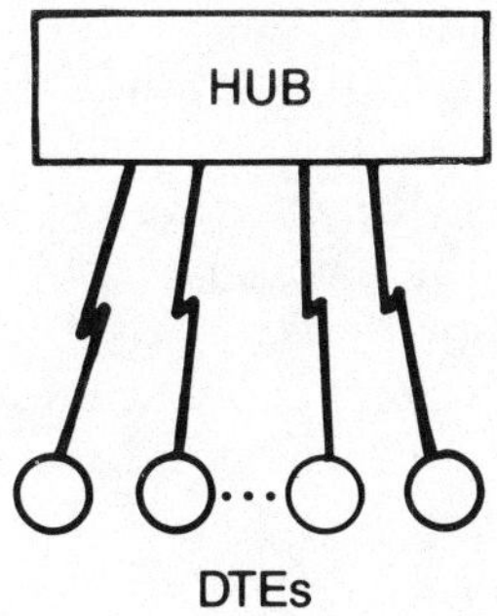

Fig 12-2
Single Hub Network

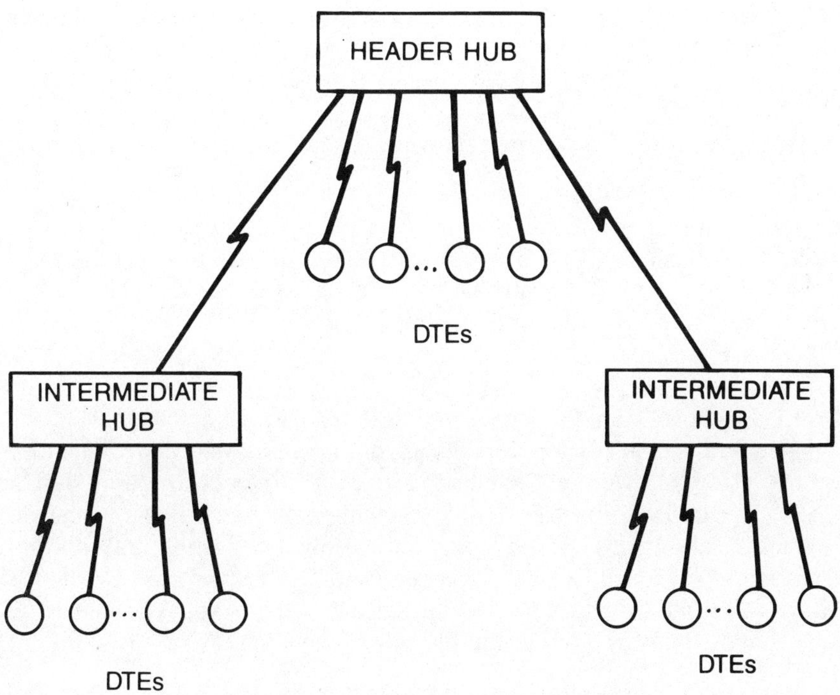

Fig 12-3
Network With Two Levels of Hubs

a hub via separate transmit and receive channels (normally two twisted pairs). An IH propagates signals from its DTEs toward the HH; it sends CP toward the HH in the event of a collision. The HH repeats the signals it receives from DTEs or IHs back down to all DTEs and IHs. The HH generates CP if more than one of its inputs becomes active. The IHs repeat the signals received from the HH, and broadcast to all the connected DTEs' receivers. Hubs do not distinguish whether input signals along the upward path emanate from DTEs or lower-level IHs. If a single input is active, the hub repeats the signal regardless of its source; if more than one is active, it generates CP.

A configuration involving four hub levels and a special link is illustrated in Fig 12-4. In this example, one IH is used for simple repeating (one connection upward and one connection downward). Other than having one link in and one link out, repeaters are identical to other hubs. Special links are connections, possibly containing active devices, that are used for situations requiring extra propagation delay or special transmission media.

12.2.2 Application Perspective. The primary application area for type 1BASE5 is expected to be in office environments for networking DTEs such as personal computers or other workstations. In many cases, spare wiring contained in existing telephone wire bundles will be used.

12.2.3 Packet Structure. Packets are transmitted from the PLS to the PMA as follows:

<silence> <preamble> <sfd> <data> <etd> <silence>

The packet elements shall have the following characteristics:

Element	Characteristics
<silence>	No transitions
<preamble>	Alternating CD1 and CD0 for ≥56 bit times (ending in CD0)
<sfd>	CD1 CD0 CD1 CD0 CD1 CD0 CD1 CD1
<data>	8 × N instances of CD0 or CD1
<etd>	First part of IDL

12.2.3.1 Silence. The <silence> delimiter provides an observation window for an unspecified period of time during which no transitions occur. The minimum duration of <etd> followed by <silence> is the interFrameGap defined in 4.4.2.2.

12.2.3.2 Preamble. The <preamble> delimiter begins a packet transmission and provides a signal for receiver synchronization. The signal shall be an alternating pattern of CD1 and CD0. This pattern shall be transmitted by the DTE for a minimum of 56 bit times at the beginning of each packet. The last bit of the preamble (that is, the final bit of preamble before the start-of-frame delimiter) shall be a CD0.

The DTE is required to supply at least 56 bits of preamble in order to satisfy system requirements. System components consume preamble bits in order to perform their functions. The number of preamble bits sourced ensures an adequate number of bits are provided to each system component to correctly implement its function.

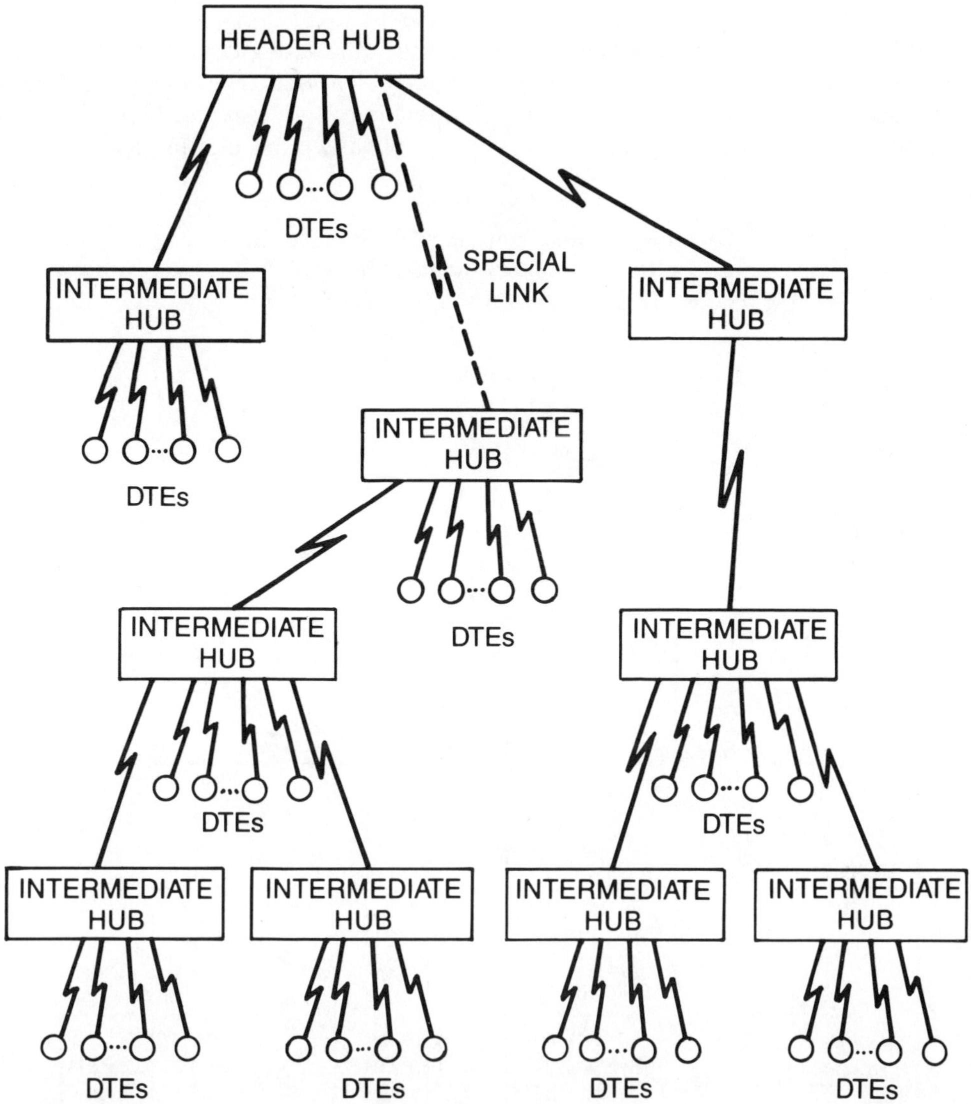

Fig 12-4
Network With Four Levels of Hubs

12.2.3.3 Start-of-Frame Delimiter. The <sfd> indicates the start of a frame, and follows the preamble.

12.2.3.4 Data. The <data> in a transmission shall be in multiples of eight (8) encoded data bits (CD0s and CD1s).

12.2.3.5 End-of-Transmission Delimiter. The <etd> indicates the end of a transmission and serves to turn off the transmitter. The signal shall be the first part of an IDL.

12.3 DTE Physical Signaling (PLS) Specification

12.3.1 Overview. This section defines logical characteristics of the DTE PLS sublayer for 1BASE5. The relationship of this specification to the entire standard is shown in Fig 12-5. The sublayer and its relationship to the MAC and PMA sublayers are described in an abstract way and do not imply any particular implementation.

Fig 12-5
Station Physical Signaling Relationship to the OSI Reference Model and the IEEE 802.3 CSMA/CD LAN Model

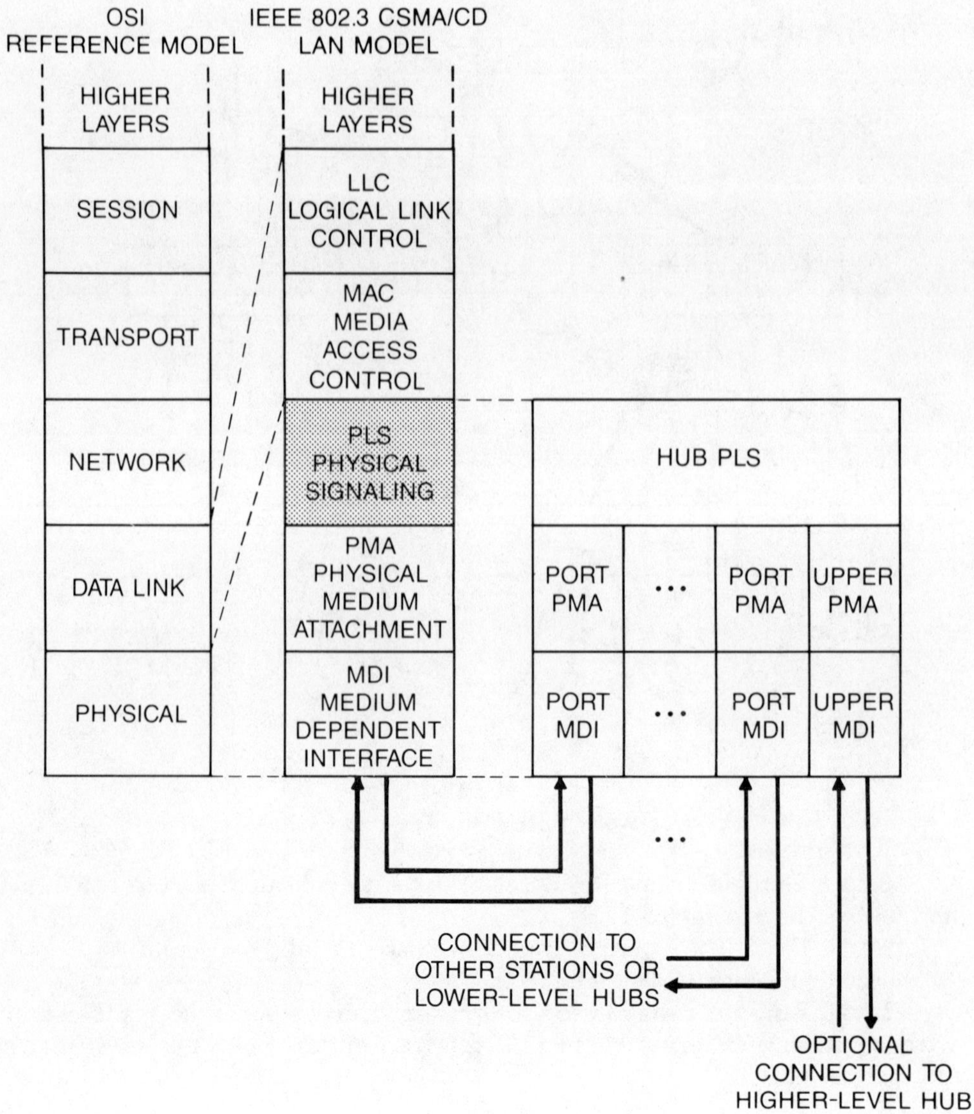

12.3.1.1 Summary of Major Concepts

(1) There are two channels between the PLS and PMA sublayers. Output data are passed through the output channel and input data and control (CP) are passed through the input channel.

(2) Each direction of data transfer through the PLS operates independently and simultaneously (that is, the PLS is full duplex).

12.3.1.2 Application Perspective. The DTE PLS sublayer performs the following functions:

(1) Encodes OUTPUT_UNITs from the MAC sublayer into a Manchester-encoded waveform that it sends to the PMA sublayer output circuit

(2) Decodes a Manchester-encoded waveform from the PMA sublayer input circuit into INPUT_UNITs, CARRIER_STATUS, and SIGNAL_STATUS

12.3.2 Functional Specification. This section provides a detailed model for the DTE PLS sublayer.

Many of the terms used in this section are specific to the interface between this sublayer and the MAC sublayer. These terms are defined in the service specification for the PLS sublayer (see 6.3).

12.3.2.1 PLS-PMA Interface. The PLS and PMA communicate by means of the following messages:

Message	Meaning	Source
output	Output information	PLS
output_idle	No data to be output	PLS
input	Input information	PMA
input_idle	No input information	PMA

12.3.2.1.1 *output* Message. The PLS sublayer sends an *output* message to the PMA sublayer when the PLS sublayer receives an OUTPUT_UNIT from the MAC sublayer.

The physical realization of the *output* message is a CD0 or a CD1 sent by the PLS to the PMA. The PLS sends a CD0 if the OUTPUT_UNIT is a ZERO or a CD1 if the OUPUT_UNIT is a ONE. This message is time-coded. That is, once this message has been sent, the function is not completed until one bit time later. The *output* message cannot be sent again until the bit cell being sent as a result of sending the previous *output* message is complete.

12.3.2.1.2 *output_idle* Message. The PLS sublayer sends an *output_idle* message to the PMA sublayer at all times when the MAC sublayer is not in the process of transferring output data across the MAC to PLS interface. The *output_idle* message is no longer sent (and the first OUTPUT_UNIT is sent using the *output* message) when the first OUTPUT_UNIT of a packet is received from the MAC sublayer. The *output_idle* message is again sent to the PMA when DATA_COMPLETE is received from the MAC sublayer.

The physical realization of the *output_idle* message is IDL sent by the PLS to the PMA.

12.3.2.1.3 *input* Message. The PMA sublayer sends an *input* message to the PLS sublayer when the PMA has received a bit from the medium and is prepared to transfer this bit to the PLS.

The physical realization of the *input* message consists of data units, CD0, CD1, CVL, or CVH, derived from the incoming data stream. If ambiguity exists due to excessive noise or jitter, the PMA may send an arbitrary combination of these.

12.3.2.1.4 *input_idle* Message. The PMA sublayer sends an *input_idle* message to the PLS sublayer when the PMA sublayer does not have data to send to the PLS sublayer. This condition exists when carrier is lost or IDL is received.

12.3.2.2 PLS-MAC Interface. The PLS and MAC communicate by means of the following messages:

Message	Meaning	Source
OUTPUT_UNIT	Data sent to the PMA	MAC
OUTPUT_STATUS	Response to OUTPUT_UNIT	PLS
INPUT_UNIT	Data received from the PMA	PLS
CARRIER_STATUS	Indication of input activity	PLS
SIGNAL_STATUS	Indication of error/no error condition	PLS

12.3.2.2.1 OUTPUT_UNIT. The MAC sublayer sends the PLS sublayer an OUTPUT_UNIT every time the MAC sublayer has a bit to send. Once the MAC sublayer has sent an OUTPUT_UNIT to the PLS sublayer, it may not send another OUTPUT_UNIT until it has received an OUTPUT_STATUS message from the PLS sublayer. The OUTPUT_UNIT is a ONE if the MAC sublayer wants the PLS sublayer to send a CD1 to the PMA sublayer, a ZERO if a CD0 is desired, or a DATA_COMPLETE if an IDL is desired.

12.3.2.2.2 OUTPUT_STATUS. The PLS sublayer sends the MAC sublayer an OUTPUT_STATUS in response to every OUTPUT_UNIT received by the PLS sublayer. OUTPUT_STATUS sent is an OUTPUT_NEXT when the PLS sublayer is ready to accept the next OUTPUT_UNIT from the MAC sublayer. (The purpose of OUTPUT_STATUS is to synchronize the MAC sublayer data output with the data rate of the physical medium.)

12.3.2.2.3 INPUT_UNIT. The PLS sublayer sends the MAC sublayer an INPUT_UNIT every time the PLS receives an *input* message from the PMA sublayer. The INPUT_UNIT is a ONE if the PLS sublayer receives a CD1 from the PMA sublayer or a ZERO if the PLS sublayer receives a CD0 from the PMA sublayer. The INPUT_UNIT may be either ZERO or ONE if the PLS sublayer receives a CVL or CVH from the PMA sublayer.

12.3.2.2.4 CARRIER_STATUS. The PLS sublayer sends the MAC sublayer CARRIER_STATUS whenever there is a change in carrier status, as detected by the PMA. The PLS sublayer sends CARRIER_ON when it receives an *input* message from the PMA and the previous CARRIER_STATUS that the PLS sublayer sent to the MAC sublayer was CARRIER_OFF. The PLS sublayer sends CARRIER_OFF when it receives an *input_idle* from the PMA sublayer, and the previous CARRIER_STATUS that the PLS sublayer sent to the MAC sublayer was CARRIER_ON.

12.3.2.2.5 SIGNAL_STATUS. The PLS sublayer sends the MAC sublayer SIGNAL_STATUS whenever it detects the beginning or end of Collision Presence. The PLS sublayer sends SIGNAL_ERROR when it receives *input* message CVL or CVH from the PMA sublayer and the previous SIGNAL_STATUS the PLS sublayer sent was NO_SIGNAL_ERROR. The PLS sublayer sends NO_SIGNAL_ERROR when it receives an *input_idle* message from the PMA sublayer and the previous SIGNAL_STATUS that the PLS sent to the MAC sublayer was SIGNAL_ERROR. The PLS shall send SIGNAL_ERROR to the MAC sublayer when the Collision Presence pattern is detected; it may send SIGNAL_ERROR any time it receives an *input* message that is neither CD0 nor CD1.

12.3.2.3 PLS Functions. The PLS sublayer functions consist of four simultaneous and asynchronous functions. These functions are Output, Input, Error Sense, and Carrier Sense. All of the four functions are started immediately following PowerOn. These functions are depicted in the state diagrams shown in Fig 12-6 through Fig 12-9, using the notation described in 1.2.1.

12.3.2.3.1 State Diagram Variables. The variables used in the state diagrams and the corresponding descriptions are the following:

(1) Inter Process Flags

disable_SIGNAL_ERROR — Used in the state diagrams and functions. It is used by the Input Function to prevent false collision detection by the Error Sense Function during preamble startup.

protectTimer — Used by the Carrier Sense Function to implement the protection period described in 12.5.3.2.3. It is started by "start_protectTimer." "protectTimer_done" is satisfied when the timer has expired.

12.3.2.3.2 Output Function. The Output Function transparently performs the task of data transfer from the MAC sublayer to the PMA sublayer. The state diagram of Fig 12-6 depicts the Output Function operation.

12.3.2.3.3 Input Function. The Input Function transparently performs the task of data transfer from the PMA sublayer to the MAC sublayer. The state diagram of Fig 12-7 depicts the Input Function operation.

12.3.2.3.4 Error Sense Function. The Error Sense Function performs the task of sending SIGNAL_STATUS to the MAC sublayer at the beginning and end of the Collision Presence pattern. The state diagram of Fig 12-8 depicts the Error Sense Function operation.

12.3.2.3.5 Carrier Sense Function. The Carrier Sense Function performs the task of sending CARRIER_STATUS to the MAC sublayer whenever the input becomes active or idle, as detected by the PMA sublayer. The state diagram of Fig 12-9 depicts the Carrier Sense Function operation.

A timer may be used by the Carrier Sense Function to implement the protection period described in 12.5.3.2.3. It is started by "start_protectTimer" and asserts "protectTimer_done" after 0 to 30 μs since starting.

12.3.2.4 Signal Encoding. Five distinct symbols can be transmitted on the line: CD0, CD1, CVL, CVH, and IDL. Of these, CVL and CVH are transmitted only as part of the collision presence reporting pattern CP.

12.3.2.4.1 Data Transmission Rate. The data transmission rate (BR) is 1 Mb/s $\pm$0.01%. A bit time (BT) is therefore nominally 1 μs.

12.3.2.4.2 Data Symbol Encoding. Manchester encoding is used for the transmission of packets. Manchester encoding is a binary signaling mechanism that combines data and clock into bit cells. Each bit cell is split into two halves with the

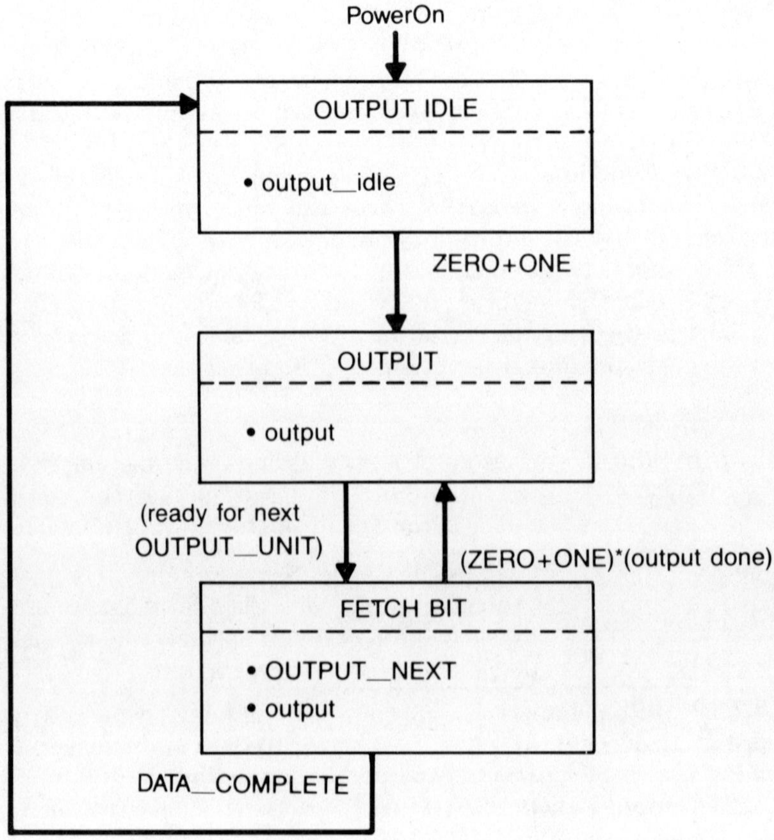

Fig 12-6
DTE PLS Output Function

second half containing the binary inverse of the first half; a transition always occurs in the middle of each bit cell. During the first half of the bit cell, the encoded signal is the logical complement of the bit value being encoded. During the second half of the bit cell, the encoded signal is the uncomplemented value of the bit being encoded. Thus, a CD0 is encoded as a bit cell in which the first half is HI and the second half is LO. A CD1 is encoded as a bit cell in which the first half is LO and the second half is HI. Examples of Manchester waveforms are shown in Fig 12-10. The zero crossings of an ideal Manchester waveform occur on precise half-bit-cell boundaries. The zero crossings of real waveforms may include timing jitter that causes deviation from these "idealized zero crossings."

12.3.2.4.3 Collision Presence Encoding. Two signals, CVL and CVH, that are transmitted only as part of the collision presence reporting pattern, CP, violate the normal Manchester encoding rule requiring a transition in the middle of each symbol. A CVH is encoded as a transition from LO to HI at the beginning of the bit cell, HI for the entire bit cell, and transition from HI to LO at the end of the bit cell.

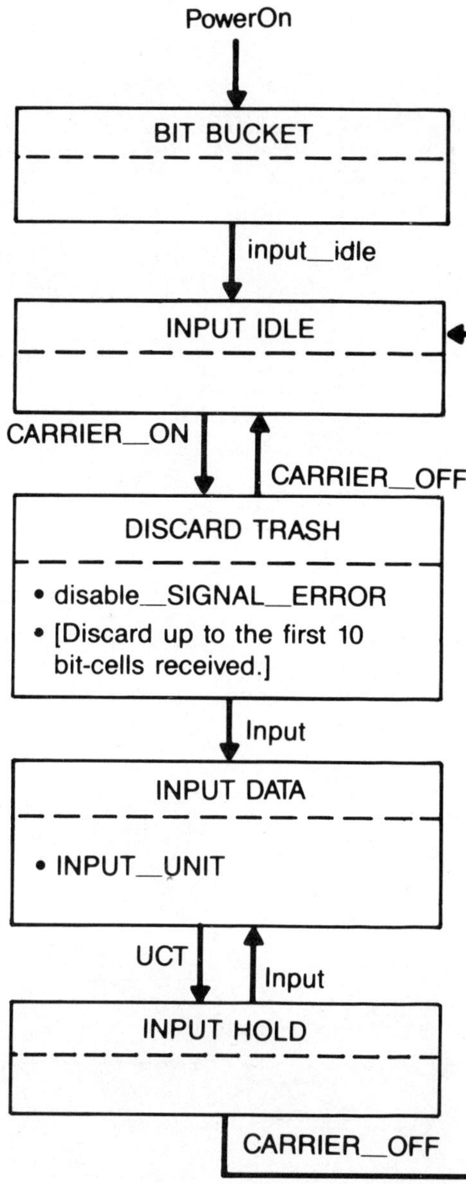

Fig 12-7
DTE PLS Input Function

A CVL is encoded as a transition from HI to LO at the beginning of the bit cell, LO for the entire bit cell, and transition from LO to HI at the end of the bit cell.

The Collision Presence reporting signal, CP, is a special sequence that differs from any legitimate Manchester-encoded signal. CP is encoded as a repeating sequence of 1 bit time LO, 1/2 bit time HI, 1 bit time LO, 1 bit time HI, 1/2 bit time LO, and

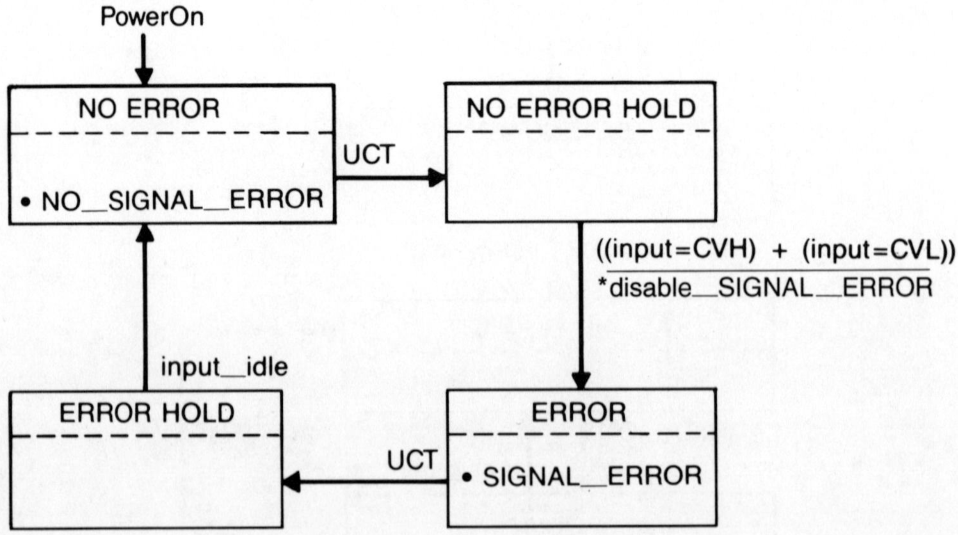

Fig 12-8
DTE PLS Error Sense Function

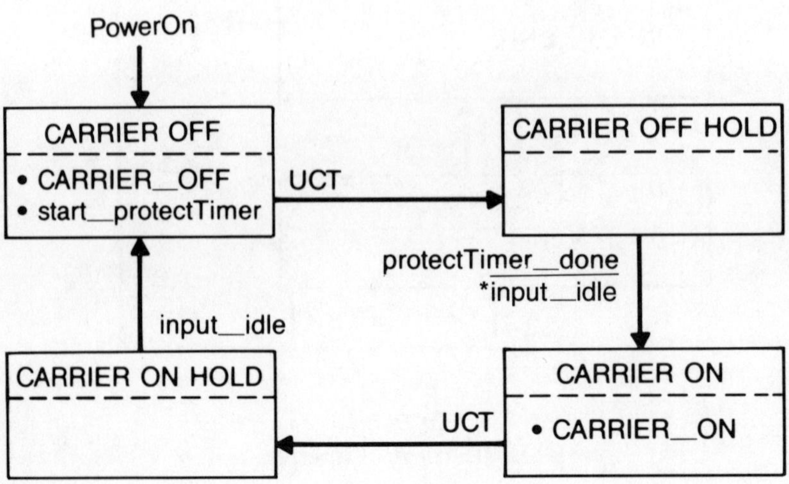

Fig 12-9
DTE PLS Carrier Sense Function

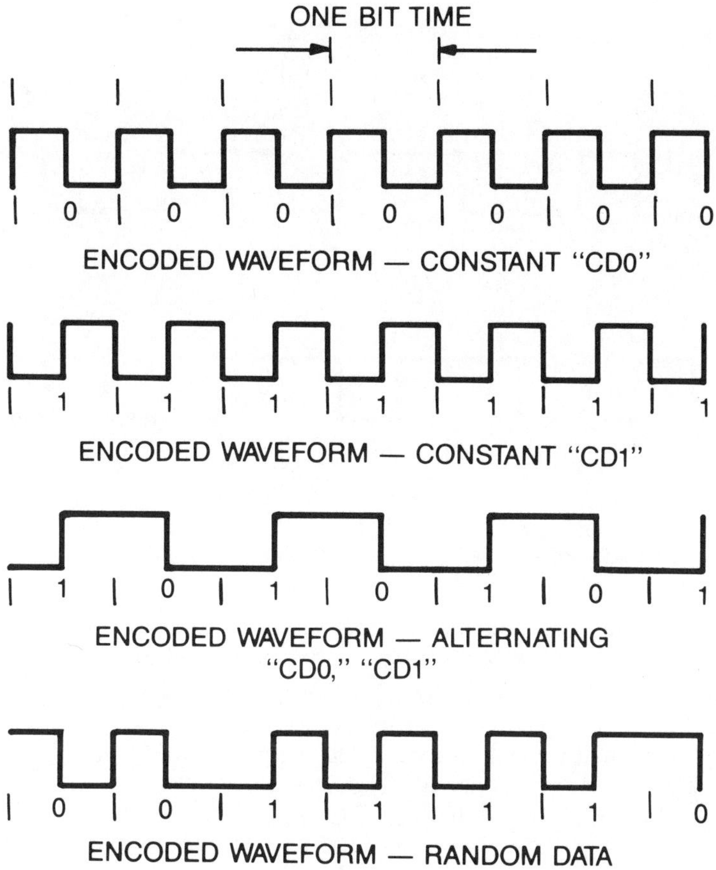

Fig 12-10
Examples of Manchester Waveforms

1 bit time HI. This may also be interpreted as repetitions of the five-symbol sequence CVL, CD0, CD1, CD0, CVH. Should a transmitter's or receiver's timing be shifted by 1/2 bit time, then the same sequence will be interpretable as repetitions of CD1, CVL, CVH, CD1, CD0. In either case, the presence of non-Manchester symbols distinguishes the sequence from data. Examples of Collision Presence waveforms are shown in Fig 12-11. See 12.3.2.2.5 and 12.4.3.2 for further details on the detection and generation of CP.

NOTE: CP is the minimal length sequence that meets the following design criteria:

(1) The sequence should not look like legitimate Manchester-encoded data even if the receiver does not lock onto the correct bit-cell boundaries.

(2) The sequence should maintain overall dc balance. That is, it should be HI 50% of the time and LO the other 50%.

(3) The signal should occupy the same part of the frequency spectrum as normal data. That is, transitions should occur every half or whole bit time so that the fundamental signaling frequencies of BR/2 and BR are maintained. Furthermore, allowing more than one bit time to pass without a transition would introduce ambiguity with the idle line condition (IDL).

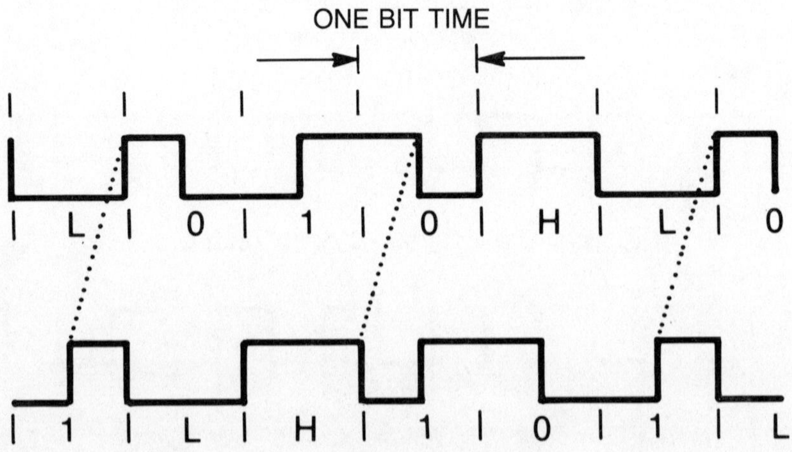

Fig 12-11
Examples of Collision Presence Waveforms

12.3.2.4.4 Idle Line Encoding. The line condition IDL is also used as an encoded signal. An IDL always starts with a HI signal level. Since IDL always starts with a HI signal, an additional transition will be added to the data stream if the last bit sent was a zero. This transition cannot be confused with clocked data (CD0 or CD1) since the transition will occur at the start of a bit cell. There will be no transition in the middle of the bit cell. The HI signal level, as sent by a transmitter, shall be maintained for a minimum of 2 bit times.

12.4 Hub Specification

12.4.1 Overview. This section defines the logical characteristics of the hub used in 1BASE5. The relationship of this specification to the entire standard is shown in Fig 12-12.

12.4.1.1 Summary of Major Concepts

(1) A hub consists of a Hub PLS sublayer and a number of instances of the PMA sublayer.

(2) One instance of the PMA sublayer, the "upper PMA," provides a connection to a higher-level hub. This PMA is not required for the header hub.

(3) Each of the remaining instances of the PMA sublayer, called "port PMAs," provides a connection to a DTE or a lower-level hub.

(4) The Hub PLS transfers data in two directions: upward from the port PMAs to the upper PMA and downward from the upper PMA to the port PMAs.

(5) The upward and downward "sides" of the hub operate independently and simultaneously.

12.4.1.2 Application Perspective. The hub is a physical layer entity that performs two functions:

(1) It retransmits incoming signals with amplitude and timing restored.

(2) It detects collisions between any two or more ports and reports knowledge of the collision by transmitting a special collision presence reporting pattern.

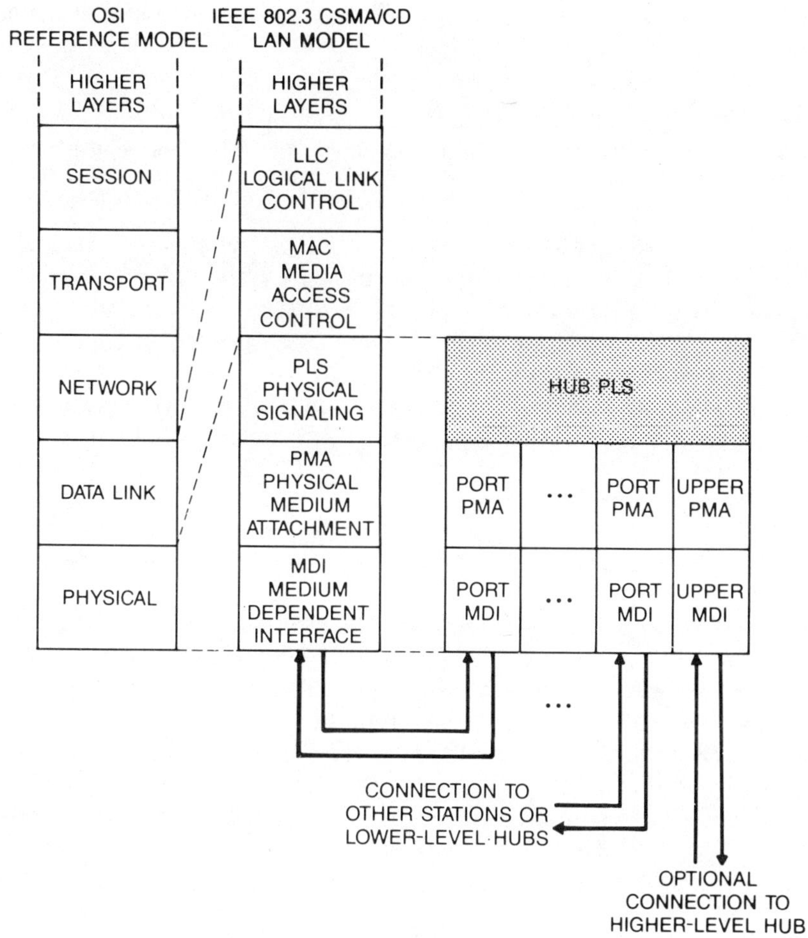

Fig 12-12
Hub Relationship to the OSI Reference Model and the IEEE 802.3 CSMA/CD LAN Model

12.4.2 Hub Structure. Each hub is functionally divided into two parts: the upward side and the downward side. The upward side is responsible for combining the transmissions from DTEs and hubs lower in the network into a single transmission to the next level up. The downward side is responsible for distributing the combined signal (which is wrapped around from the upward side of the header hub) to each of the DTEs and hubs below. Except as specified in 12.4.3.2.3 and 12.4.3.2.6, the two sides function independently.

There is an upward input channel and a corresponding downward output channel for each DTE or hub immediately below the hub. Although there is no electrical connection between the two lines, they do share a connector and cable (see 12.6 and 12.7) and are collectively known as a hub port. Each port is accessed through an instance of the PMA sublayer referred to as a "port PMA."

The one output channel from the upward side and the one input channel to the downward side of a hub are similarly paired and, for all but the header hub, are connected to a port of the next-higher-level hub. They are accessed through an instance of the PMA sublayer referred to as the "upper PMA."

NOTE: A hub that includes n hub ports should be called an n-port hub, even though it may have an extra jack for the upper PMA. The latter connection should never be counted as a port, despite common engineering usage, because it does not meet the specific definition of a 1BASE5 hub port given above.

12.4.2.1 Upward Side. The primary function of the upward side of a hub is to propagate signals from each of its inputs to its single output. If more than one input is active, then the Collision Presence signal CP is transmitted instead. In addition, the signals are retimed to restore the transitions to half-bit-time boundaries; see 12.4.3.2.5 for the details of retiming.

12.4.2.2 Downward Side. The primary function of the downward side of a hub is to repeat signals from its one input to each of its outputs. In addition, the signals are retimed to restore the transitions to half-bit-time boundaries; see 12.4.3.2.5 for the details of retiming.

12.4.3 Hub PLS Functional Specification. This section provides a detailed model for the Hub PLS sublayer.

12.4.3.1 Hub PLS to PMA Interface. The interface between the Hub PLS and the PMA is the same as that specified in 12.3.2.1 for use between the DTE PLS and the PMA except that the *output* message from the Hub PLS to the PMA is used to transmit CVL and CVH in addition to CD0 and CD1.

12.4.3.2 Hub PLS Functions. The Hub PLS sublayer functions consist of three asynchronous functions. These functions are Upward Transfer, Jabber, and Downward Transfer. All three functions are started immediately following PowerOn; an independent copy of the Jabber function is started for each port PMA. These functions are depicted in the state diagrams shown in Fig 12-13 through Fig 12-15, using the notation described in 1.2.1.

12.4.3.2.1 State Diagram Variables. The variables used in the state diagrams and the corresponding descriptions are the following:

(1) Port Designators: Instances of the PMA sublayer are referred to by index. PMA information is obtained by replacing the X in the desired function with the index of the PMA of interest. Furthermore, PMAs may be referenced by several special designators used as indices:

X	Generic port PMA designator. When X is used in a state diagram its value indicates the particular instance of a generic function.
UPPER	Indicates the upper PMA.
ALLPORTS	Indicates that all port PMAs are to be considered. All port PMAs must meet a test condition in order for that test to pass.
ALLENABLEDPORTS	Indicates that all port PMAs that are not disabled by the Jabber Function are to be considered. All such port

	PMAs must meet a test condition in order for that test to pass.
ONEPORT	Indicates that all port PMAs that are not disabled by the Jabber Function are to be considered. One, but not more than one, such port PMA must meet a test condition in order for that test to pass.
>ONEPORT	Indicates that all port PMAs that are not disabled by the Jabber Function are to be considered. Two or more such port PMAs must meet a test condition in order for that test to pass.
N	Defined by the PORT function on exiting from the UPWARD IDLE state of Fig 12-13. It indicates which port PMA caused the exit from the UPWARD IDLE state.

(2) Port Functions:

PORT(TestCondition)	Returns the index of a port PMA passing the indicated test condition. If multiple port PMAs meet the test condition, the PORT function will return one and only one of the acceptable values.

(3) Input Variables:

INPUT(X)	Indicates the state of activity on the designated PMA input channel. It may be either "idle" or "active." The former indicates that *input_idle* is asserted; the latter indicates that it is not asserted.
input(X)	Used to receive an *input* message (see 12.3.2.1) from the designated PMA input channel.
probation_alternative	Used to distinguish between the two allowed alternatives for exiting the JABBER JAM state of Fig 12-14 when an active port becomes idle. The implementor of a hub may treat the variable as either true or false.

(4) Output Variables:

output(X)	Used to send an *output* message (see 12.3.2.1 and 12.4.3.1) to the designated PMA output channel.
output_idle(X)	Used to send an *output_idle* message (see 12.3.2.1) on the designated PMA output channel.

(5) Inter Process Flags:

send_collision	Used by the Upward Signal Transfer Function to indicate a series of *output* messages to the upper PMA sublayer, the effect of which is to transmit the CP signal, as described in 12.3.2.4.2, 12.3.2.4.3, and 12.4.3.2.7.

jabber_collision — Used by the various instances of the Jabber Function to signal the Upward Signal Transfer Function that CP should be generated.

disable_input(X) — Used to disable the designated PMA input channel. The input is reenabled when disable_input(X) is no longer asserted. Only the Upward Signal Transfer Function is affected by the disabling of a port (via the ALLENABLEDPORTS, ONEPORT, and >ONEPORT designators).

jabberTime1 — Used by the Jabber Function (see 12.4.3.2.3) to detect excessively long transmissions. It is started by "start_jabberTime1." "jabberTime1_done" is satisfied when the timer has expired.

jabberTime2 — Used by the Jabber Function (see 12.4.3.2.3) to determine when to disable ports due to excessively long transmissions. It is started by "start_jabberTime2." "jabberTime2_done" is satisfied when the timer has expired.

12.4.3.2.2 Upward Signal Transfer Function. The Upward Signal Transfer Function combines signals from the various port inputs and passes them on to the upper output. It also detects and reports collisions as appropriate. The state diagram of Fig 12-13 depicts its operation.

Signals are propagated upward according to the following rules, except as controlled by the Jabber Function (see 12.4.3.2.3):

(1) If IDL is present on all port inputs, then transmit IDL.

(2) If IDL is present on all but one of the port inputs, then repeat the signal received from that one line. If that one signal is CP, then a hub may generate its own CP signal instead of repeating the received CP signal.

(3) If two or more inputs are active (non-IDL) at the same time, then transmit CP and continue transmitting CP until all inputs indicate IDL again.

Whenever the hub finishes transmitting CP, it shall then transmit IDL, including the extended HI period.

12.4.3.2.3 Jabber Function. The Jabber Function detects abnormally long transmissions and takes appropriate action to abort them. The state diagram of Fig 12-14 depicts its operation.

Two timers are used by the Jabber Function. They may be implemented either as local timers for each instance of the Jabber Function or as global timers shared by all instances. Futhermore, because the two timers are always started concurrently, an implementation may share circuitry between the two.

The first timer is started by "start_jabberTime1" and asserts "jabberTime1_done" after 25 to 50 ms since starting. If implemented as a single global timer, assertion of start_jabberTime1 by any instance of the Jabber Function with any other instance(s) still waiting for that timer shall not restart the timer, thereby shortening the waiting period for the latest instance.

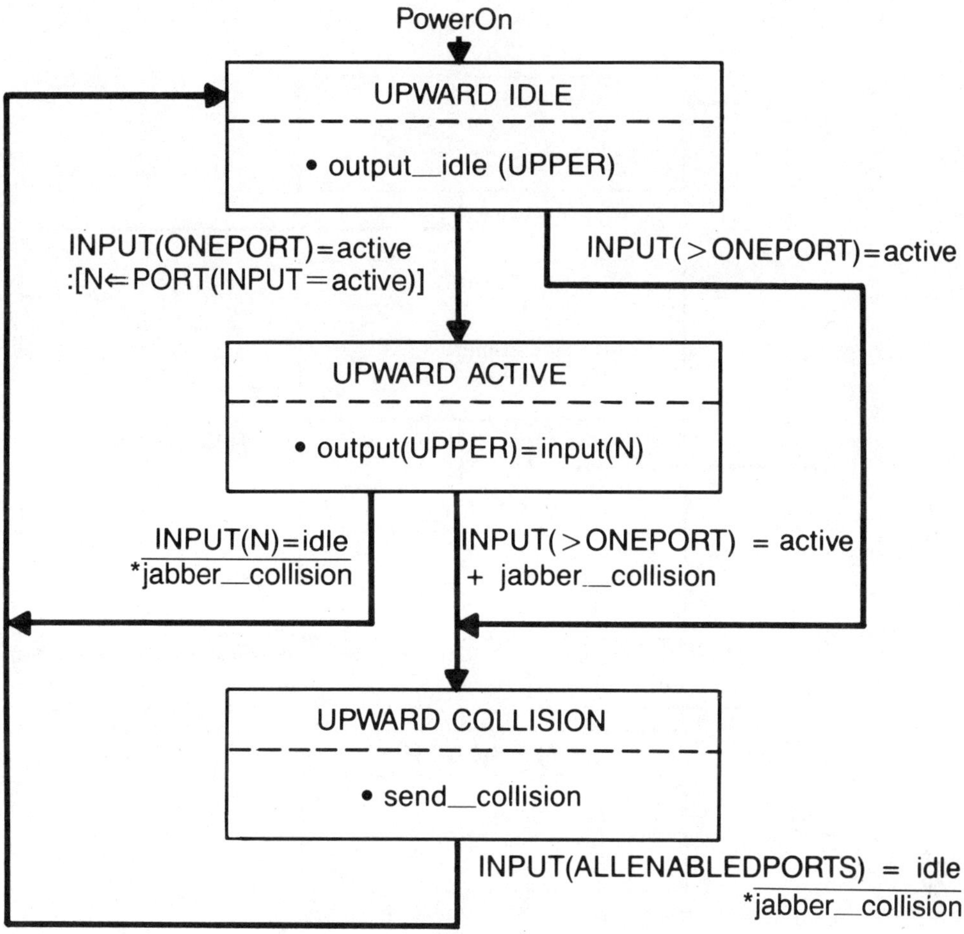

Fig 12-13
Hub PLS Upward Transfer Function

Similarly, the second timer is started by "start_jabberTime2" and asserts "jabberTime2_done" after 51 to 100 ms since starting. If implemented as a single global timer, assertion of start_jabberTime2 by any instance of the Jabber Function with any other instance(s) still waiting for that timer shall not restart the timer, thereby shortening the waiting period for the latest instance. Furthermore, if this second timer is implemented as a single global timer, then assertion of start_jabberTime1 by any instance of the Jabber Function with any other instance(s) still waiting for just the second timer (in the JABBER JAM state) shall be treated as if the first timer expires immediately (asserting jabberTime1_done) for the latest instance, thereby causing that instance to join the other instance(s) waiting for the second timer.

Hardware within the upward side of a hub shall provide a window of 25 to 50 ms, during which time a normal packet or CP sequence may be propagated upward. If

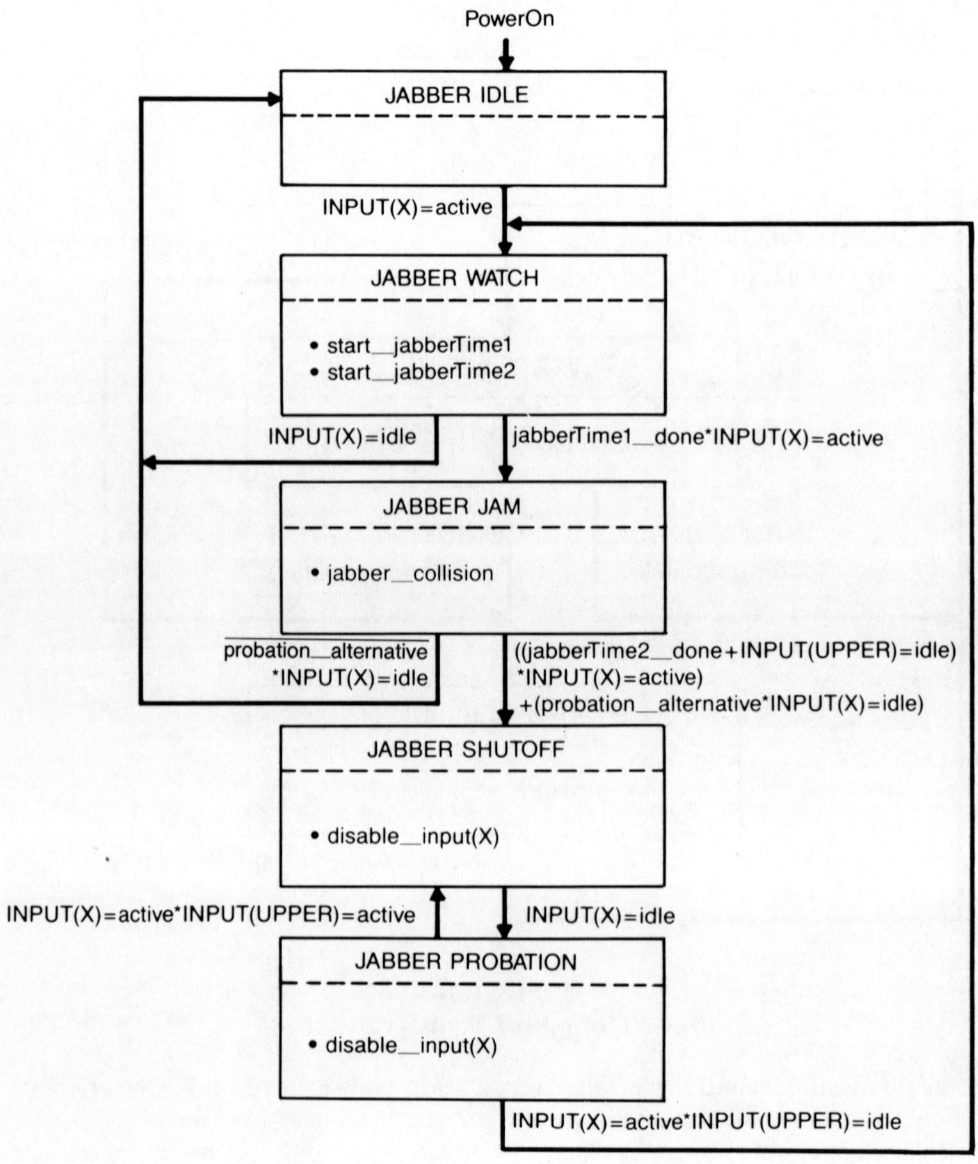

Fig 12-14
Hub PLS Jabber Function for Port X

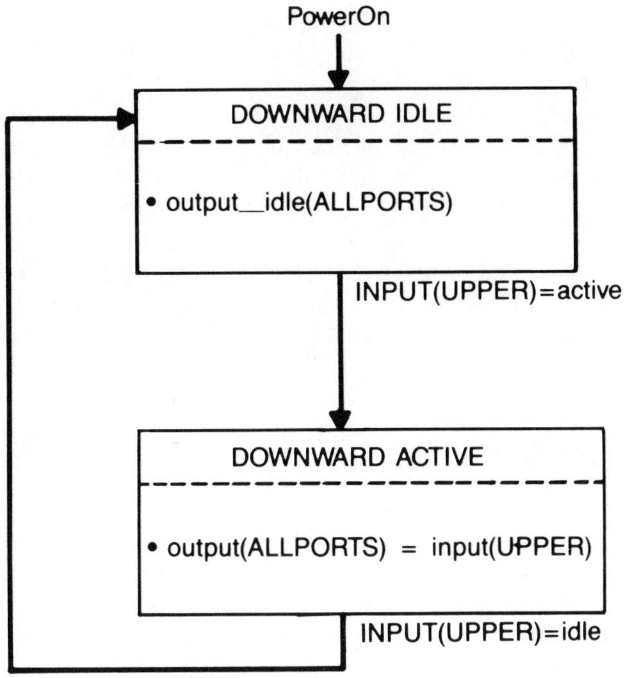

Fig 12-15
Hub PLS Downward Transfer Function

any port input (or, as an alternative implementation, the hub's combined upward signal) exceeds this duration without becoming idle, then the hub shall switch to transmitting CP until 51 to 100 ms after the beginning of the window and then, if that input is still active, disable that input (or all nonidle inputs) until it once again becomes active while the downward side is idle.

The "probation_alternative" input variable is used to distinguish between the two allowed alternatives for exiting the JABBER JAM state of Fig 12-14 when an active port becomes idle. The implementor of a hub may treat the variable as either true or false. If true, the port will enter the JABBER PROBATION state (via the JABBER SHUTOFF state); if false, the port will instead return to the JABBER IDLE state.

12.4.3.2.4 Downward Signal Transfer Function. The Downward Signal Transfer Function repeats signals from the upper input to the various port outputs. The state diagram of Fig 12-15 depicts its operation.

The downward side of a hub may detect the Collision Presence signal at the upper input and generate its own CP signal to be transmitted at the port outputs (in place of repeating the received CP signal).

Whenever the hub finishes transmitting CP, it shall then transmit IDL, including the extended HI period.

12.4.3.2.5 Retiming (Jitter Removal). Each side of each hub shall retime any clocked signals that it propagates so that the transitions occur on half-bit-time boundaries, thereby avoiding accumulation of excessive jitter. Such retiming shall preserve the sequence of CD0, CD1, CVL, and CVH symbols being propagated.

If an ambiguity exists in the incoming bit cells due to excessive noise or jitter, then the appropriate side of the hub may either switch to generating CP or replace the erroneous bit cell with an arbitrary combination of half or whole bit cells.

Retiming also accounts for differences (if any) in clock rates between that used to send bit cells to the hub and that used to send them out from the hub. Excessive differences in clock rates (caused by clocks not meeting 12.3.2.4.1) and excessively long packets (caused by exceeding maxFrameSize) may each cause the capacity of the retiming function to be exceeded. In such circumstances, the appropriate side of the hub may either switch to transmitting CP or add or delete half or whole bit cells as needed.

Whenever bit cells are added, deleted, or replaced, the hub shall maintain synchronization of the outgoing bit cells to a half or whole bit cell boundary. Furthermore, it shall not generate periods of more than one bit time without a transition.

12.4.3.2.6 Header Hub Wrap-Around. For each particular network configuration, one hub operates as the header hub and all others as intermediate hubs. It is suggested, but not required, that hub implementations be capable of being used for either purpose. Methods for switching between these two modes are beyond the scope of this standard.

For an intermediate hub, the upper output shall be connected to a port input of the next higher-level hub and the upper input shall be connected to a port output of a higher-level hub.

For the header hub, the upper output shall be connected to the upper input. This wrap-around may appropriately bypass parts of the PMA specification so long as the resulting implementation is functionally equivalent to one with a wired connection. For example, signals internal to the hub need not be translated to the corresponding external levels and then translated back to internal levels. Similarly, it shall not be necessary to retime the wrapped signal twice, once in the upward side and then again in the downward side of the same header hub; a single retiming is permissible.

12.4.3.2.7 Collision Presence Startup. When a hub starts generating CP (as specified in 12.4.3.2.2 through 12.4.3.2.5) it shall synchronize the startup to a half or whole bit-cell boundary of any immediately preceding signal. If it was sending IDL immediately before the CP, no synchronization or preamble is required.

A hub may start transmission of CP at any point in the sequence that does not result in periods of more than one bit time without a transition during the switch from passing on data to sending CP. Depending on the preceding signal, it may start with L010H, 010HL, 10HL0, 0HL01, or HL010. Because startup may be synchronized to any half-bit-cell boundary, a hub may also transmit the shifted version of CP starting with 1LH10, LH101, H101L, 101LH, or 01LH1.

12.4.3.3 Reliability. Hubs shall be designed to provide a mean time between failure (MTBF) of at least 45 000 hours of operation. Hubs, including the associated connectors and other passive components, should be designed to minimize the probability that a particular failure results in total network failure. Furthermore, the port electronics of each hub should be designed so as to minimize the probability that the failure of one port prevents communication by equipment attached to the other ports.

12.5 Physical Medium Attachment (PMA) Specification

12.5.1 Overview. This section defines the Physical Medium Attachment (PMA) sublayer for 1BASE5. The relationship of this specification to the entire standard is shown in Fig 12-16. The PMA sublayer connects the PLS sublayer to the Medium Dependent Interface (MDI).

12.5.2 PLS-PMA Interface. The interface between the PLS and the PMA sublayers is specified in 12.3.2.1 for DTEs and in 12.4.3.1 for hubs.

12.5.3 Signal Characteristics

12.5.3.1 Transmitter Characteristics. Transmitters should operate properly when loaded with any cable meeting the requirements of 12.7. To approximate the boundary conditions of such loading, two specific test loads are specified. Transmitters shall meet all requirements of this section when connected to both the "light" (115 Ω) load shown in Fig 12-17 and the "heavy" (approximately 80 Ω) load shown in Fig 12-18. It is expected that transmitters that perform correctly with these two loads will also perform acceptably under intermediate loading conditions.

12.5.3.1.1 Differential Output Voltage. For simplicity of explanation, the text and figures of this section describe the differential output voltage in terms of voltage magnitudes. The requirements of this section apply to the negative pulses as well as the positive ones.

Beginning with the second bit of the preamble (or CP, if no preamble is present), pulses of duration BT/2 shall meet the conditions of Fig 12-19. Pulses of duration BT shall meet the conditions of Fig 12-20. After the zero-crossing, the output shall exceed the voltage of a signal rising from the zero-crossing to 2.0 V with a slope of magnitude 20 mV/ns. The output shall remain above 2.0 V until 100 ns before the next zero-crossing. The peak output voltage shall not exceed 3.65 V. While falling from 2.0 V to the zero-crossing, the signal shall exceed the voltage of a signal falling from 2.0 V to the zero-crossing with a slope of magnitude 20 mV/ns.

For pulses of duration BT, the average voltage that appears from 100 ns after the zero-crossing through BT/2 shall be between 0.95 and 1.8 times the average voltage that appears from time BT/2 through 100 ns before the following zero-crossing. Similarly, for pulses of duration BT, the peak voltage that appears from 100 ns after the zero-crossing through BT/2 shall be between 0.95 and 1.8 times the peak voltage that appears from time BT/2 through 100 ns before the following zero-crossing.

NOTE: The purpose of the above restrictions on average and peak voltages is to avoid transmitter waveforms that peak excessively during the second half of signals of duration BT, resulting in excessive jitter at the receiver. Some equalization to produce slight droop in the second half of signals of duration BT, on the other hand, may help decrease jitter at the far end of long cables.

The amplitude of the power spectrum at the output of the transmitter for all possible sequences of signals shall not exceed that produced by an idealized transmitter sending corresponding rectangular waveforms with magnitude 3.65 V at any frequency.

When a transmitter enters the idle state, it shall maintain a minimum differential output voltage of 2.0 V from 100 ns through 2BT after the last low-to-high transi-

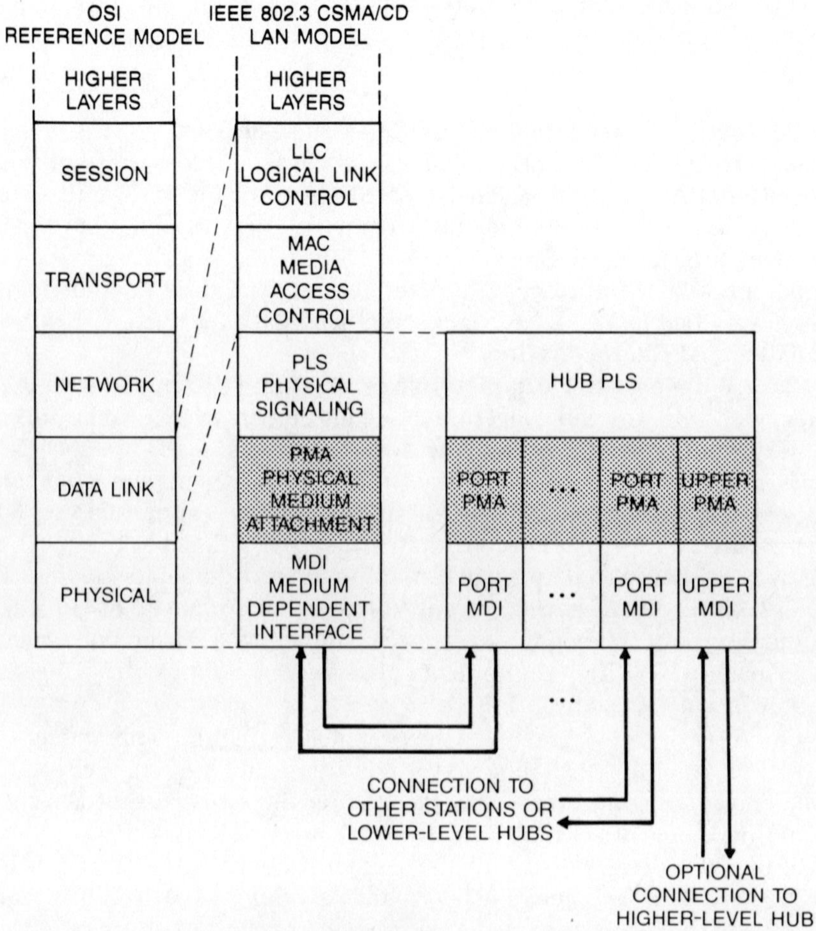

Fig 12-16
Physical Medium Attachment Relationship to the OSI Reference Model and the IEEE 802.3 CSMA/CD LAN Model

tion, as illustrated in Fig 12-21. The differential output voltage shall then fall to 1.1 V within 3BT after that same low-to-high transition. Starting when the differential output voltage first reaches 1.1 V, the magnitude of the output voltage driven into the test loads indicated in Figs 12-22 and 12-23 shall then remain within the limits indicated in Fig 12-21 until the transmitter leaves the idle state.

The transmitter output at the start of idle may exhibit overshoot, ringing, slow voltage decay, or a combination thereof due to the following factors:

(1) Change in transmitter source impedance between the active and idle states

(2) Difference in the magnitudes of the differential output voltage between the high and low output states (ΔV_{OD})

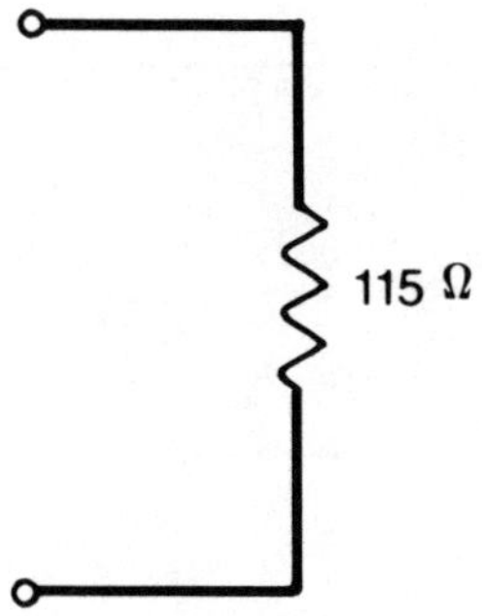

Fig 12-17
Simulated Light Load

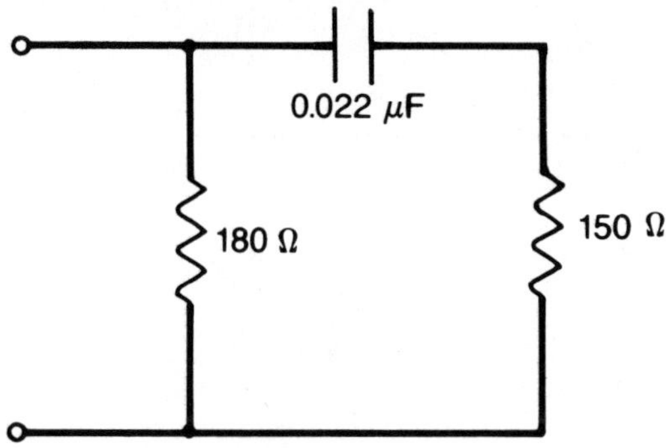

Fig 12-18
Simulated Heavy Load

(3) Waveform asymmetry at the transmitter (ΔT)
(4) Transmitter and receiver (transformer) inductance (L)

NOTE: The contribution to the undershoot from each of these can be computed with the following equations:

$V_{\Delta V_{OD}} = \pm \Delta V_{OD} \cdot R_{OFF}/2R_{ON}$
$V_{\Delta T} = (\pm \Delta T/1000\text{ ns}) \cdot V_P \cdot R_{OFF}/R_{ON}$
$V_L = -V_P \cdot (1 - e^{-2.75\,\mu s/(L_P/R_{ON})}) \cdot R_{OFF}/R_{ON}$

where:

$R_{OFF} = R_{SRC\text{-}OFF} \| R_L$
$R_{ON} = R_{SRC\text{-}ON} \| R_L$
$R_{SRC\text{-}OFF}$ = source impedance (Ω) when the driver is off
$R_{SRC\text{-}ON}$ = source impedance (Ω) when the driver is on
R_L = load impedance (Ω)
L_P = combined inductance (μH) of the transmitter and receiver transformers
ΔV_{OD} = difference (V) in magnitude of the HI and LO output voltages
ΔT = asymmetry of the waveform equals the difference between the average HI and average LO pulse widths (ns) at the transmitter
V_P = maximum output voltage (V) during the start of IDL

NOTE: The waveform shown in Fig 12-21 and the equations in the preceding note apply to a transmitter connected to the test loads of Figs 12-22 and 12-23. An actual receiver may present a more complex termination impedance and so the undershoot or overshoot may exceed that encountered with the test loads.

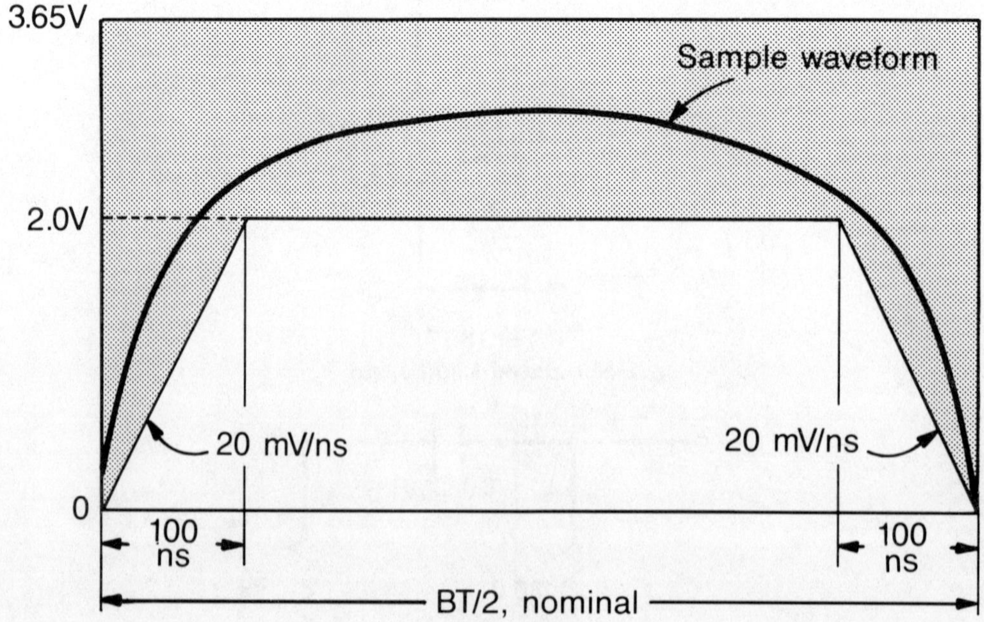

Fig 12-19
Differential Output Voltage, Nominal Duration BT/2

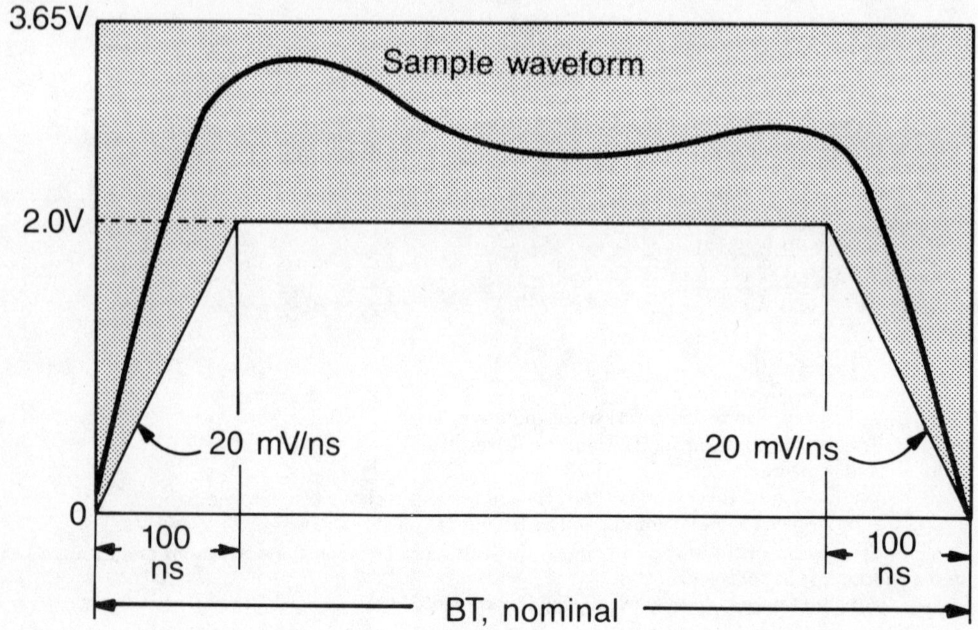

Fig 12-20
Differential Output Voltage, Duration BT

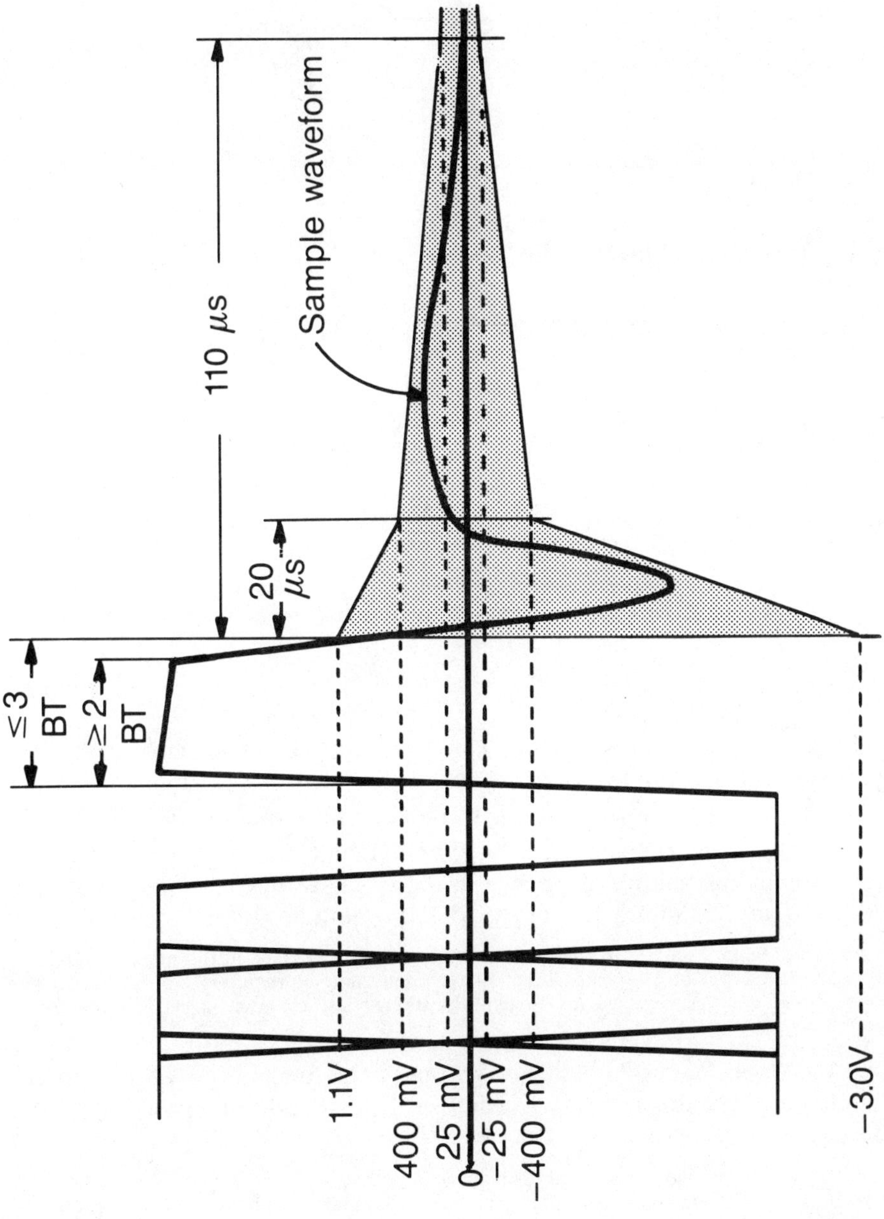

Fig 12-21
Transmitter Waveform for Idle

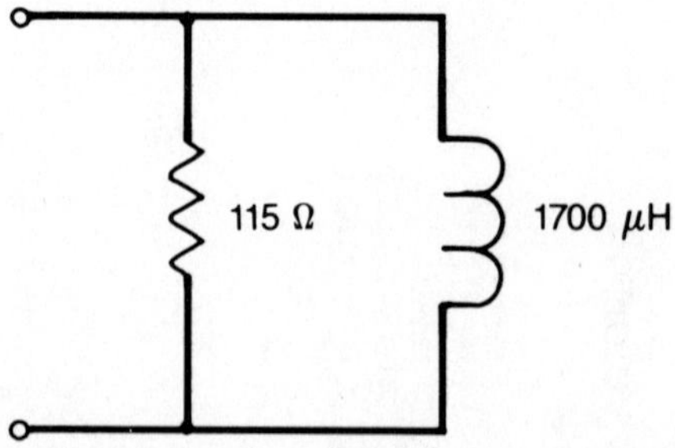

Fig 12-22
Start-of-Idle Test Load #1

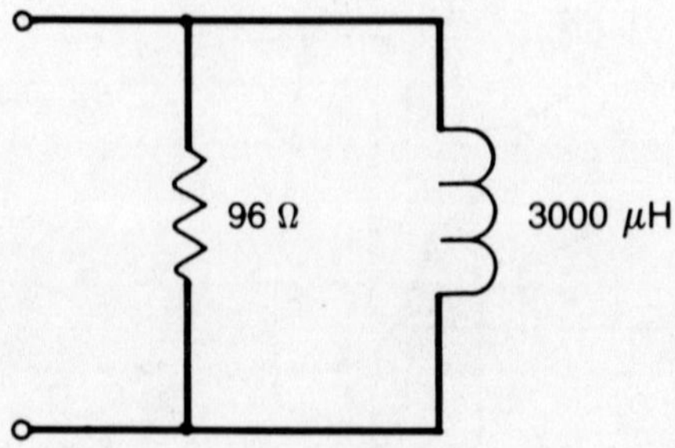

Fig 12-23
Start-of-Idle Test Load #2

12.5.3.1.2 Output Timing Jitter. The transmitted signal zero-crossings shall deviate from the idealized zero-crossings by no more than ± 10 ns.

12.5.3.1.3 Transmitter Impedance Balance. The longitudinal to metallic impedance balance of the transmitter, defined as $20 \log_{10}(E_{test}/E_{dif})$, where E_{test} is an externally applied ac voltage, as shown in Fig 12-24, shall exceed 44 dB at all frequencies up to and including 4BR in the idle and nonidle states.

NOTE: It may be difficult to measure the transmitter impedance balance in the nonidle state. A frequency-selective wavemeter or other measurement technique may be required. Furthermore, the balance of the test equipment (such as the matching of the 400 Ω resistors) must exceed that required of the transmitter.

12.5.3.1.4 Common-Mode Output Voltage. The magnitude of the total common-mode output voltage of the transmitter, E_{cm}, measured as shown in Fig 12-25, shall not exceed 300 mV.

NOTE: The implementor should consider any applicable local, national, or international regulations and standards concerning RF emission. Driving unshielded twisted pairs with high-frequency common-mode voltages may result in interference to other equipment.

12.5.3.1.5 Common-Mode Tolerance. Transmitters shall meet the requirements of 12.5.3.1.1 and 12.5.3.1.2 even in the presence of common-mode sinusoidal voltage, E_{cm} (as shown in Fig 12-26), of ± 20 V peak at frequencies from 40 kHz through 6BR.

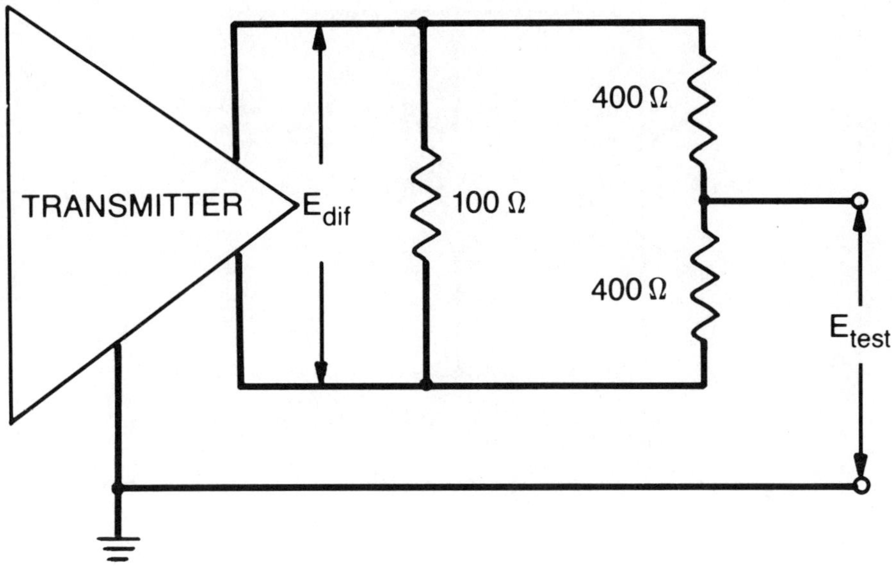

Fig 12-24
Transmitter Impedance Balance

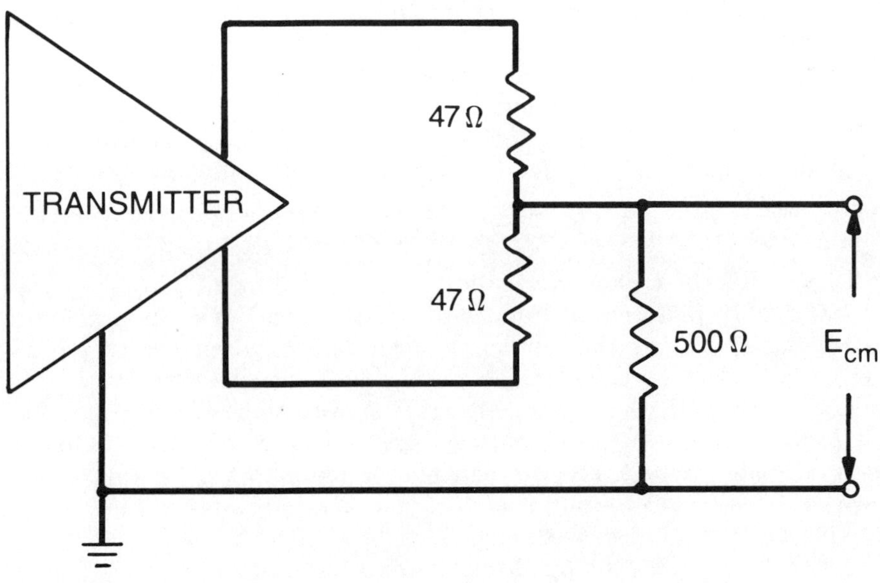

Fig 12-25
Common-Mode Output Voltage

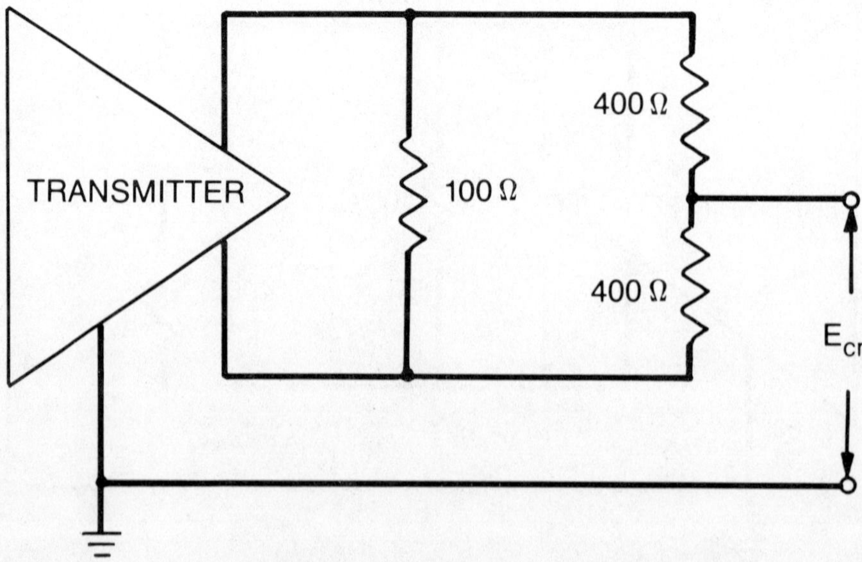

Fig 12-26
Transmitter Common-Mode Tolerance

12.5.3.1.6 Transmitter Fault Tolerance. Transmitters, both when idle and when nonidle, shall tolerate the application of short circuits across their outputs for an indefinite period of time without damage and shall resume normal operation after such faults are removed. The magnitude of the current through such a short circuit shall not exceed 300 mA.

Transmitters, both when idle and when nonidle, shall withstand, without damage, a 1000 V common-mode impulse of either polarity, applied as indicated in Fig 12-27. The shape of the impulse shall be 0.3/50 μs (300 ns virtual front time, 50 μs virtual time of half value), as defined in IEC Publication 60 (see Reference [11]).

NOTE: Tolerance of, and recovery from, the application of the telephony voltages described in 12.10.2 is optional, but the safety requirements of that section are mandatory.

12.5.3.2 Receiver Characteristics

12.5.3.2.1 Differential Input Voltage. The receiver shall operate properly when a signal meeting the minimum magnitude requirements of Fig 12-28 is received. When less than 300 mV, the magnitude of the voltage will exceed that of a straight line through the nearest zero-crossing with slope of magnitude 9 mV/ns. That is, the average slew rate near each zero-crossing will exceed 9 mV/ns. The magnitude of the voltage will also remain at or above 1.0 V for some period lasting at least 150 ns (650 ns for pulses of duration BT) that starts within 250 ns of the preceding zero-crossing and its peak will be at least 1.1 V.

12.5.3.2.2 Input Timing Jitter. Receivers shall operate properly with zero-crossing jitter of up to ±32 ns from the ideal.

12.5.3.2.3 Idle Input Behavior. The IDL condition shall be detected within 1.8 bit times of the last low-to-high transition at the receiver.

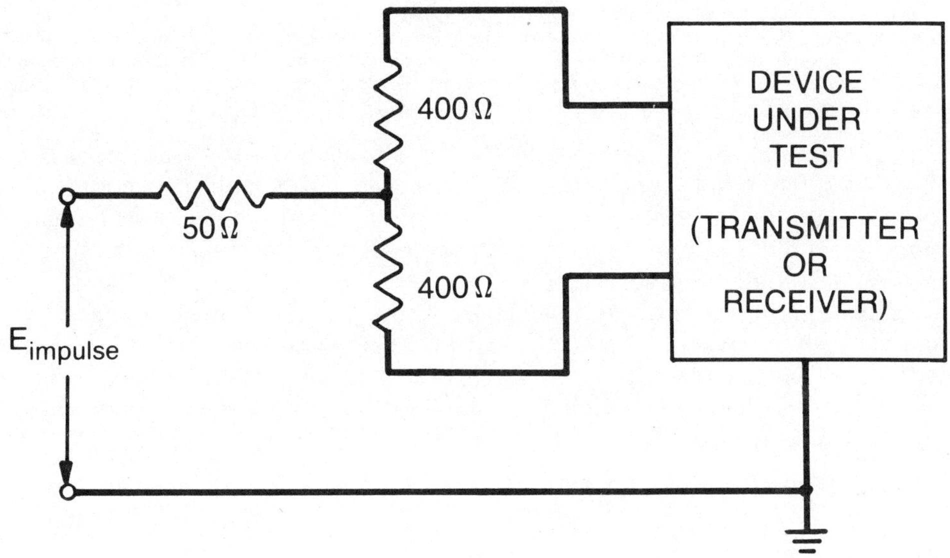

Fig 12-27
Common-Mode Impulse Test

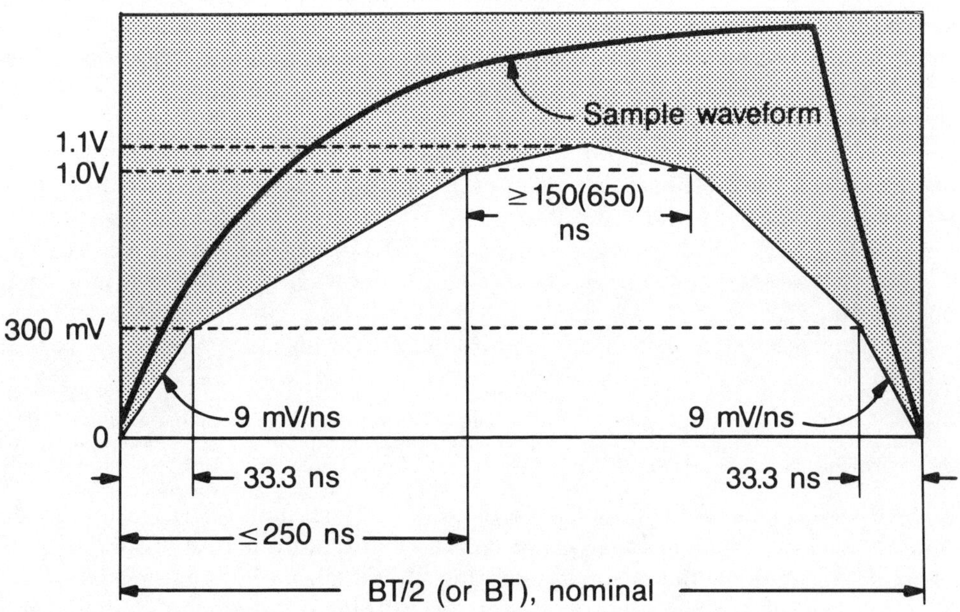

Fig 12-28
Receiver Signal Envelope

NOTE: (1) It is necessary to distinguish CVH from IDL.

(2) System jitter considerations make it impractical to detect IDL (<etd>, end-of-transmission delimiter) any sooner than 1.3 bit times. The specific implementation of the clock recovery mechanism, or equivalent, determines the lower bound on the actual IDL detection time. Adequate margin should be provided between the lower bound and 1.8 bit times.

The receiver shall take precautions to ensure that the HI-to-silence transition of the start of IDL is not falsely interpreted as a silence-to-nonidle transition, even in the presence of signal droop, overshoot, ringing, slow voltage decay, or a combination thereof due to capacitive and inductive effects in the transmitter, cable, and receiver, including those discussed in 12.5.3.1.1.

To this end, a receiver in a hub shall treat its input as if it were idle for between 20 and 30 μs after detecting IDL. The timing of this "protection" period for the port PMAs may use a single timer that is started when all ports have become idle or disabled by the Jabber Function. Receivers in DTEs may include a similar protection period of up to 30 μs.

NOTE: The protection period is required in hubs because erroneously interpreting the start-of-idle as a new transmission will result in propagation of the error to DTEs, despite any precautions taken in those DTEs. The protection period is optional in DTEs because any implementation error in a DTE will affect only that particular DTE.

12.5.3.2.4 Differential Input Impedance. The (complex) differential input impedance of the receiver, $Z_{receiver}$, shall be such that the reflection attenuation, defined as $20 \log_{10}(|Z_{receiver} + Z_{cable}| / |Z_{receiver} - Z_{cable}|)$, where Z_{cable} is the differential characteristic impedance of the attached cable, exceeds 16 dB over the range BR/2 through 2BR for all cables meeting the requirements of 12.7.2.

12.5.3.2.5 Common-Mode Rejection. Receivers shall assume the proper output state for any differential input signal, E_s, that results in a signal, E_{dif}, that meets 12.5.3.2.1 and 12.5.3.2.2, even in the presence of common-mode sinusoidal, voltages, E_{cm} (as shown in Fig 12-29), of ± 20 V peak at frequencies from 40 kHz through 6BR.

12.5.3.2.6 Noise Immunity. Receivers shall meet the following limits on average error rates when the noise described in 12.7.4 is added to the signals described in 12.5.3.2.1 and 12.5.3.2.2:

(1) When nonidle, the receiver error rate shall not exceed one error in 10^8 bits.

(2) When idle, a receiver used in a DTE shall not falsely detect carrier more than once in 100 s.

(3) When idle, a receiver used in a hub shall not falsely detect carrier more than once in 1500 s.

NOTE: Receivers whose inputs include a 2-4 MHz, 2-pole, low-pass, Butterworth filter and a 560 mV squelch level will meet this last requirement for idle-mode noise immunity yet still perform properly with the weakest signal allowed by 12.5.3.2.1.

12.5.3.2.7 Receiver Fault Tolerance. Receivers shall tolerate the application of short circuits across their inputs for an indefinite period of time without damage and shall resume normal operation after such faults are removed.

Receivers shall withstand, without damage, a 1000 V common-mode impulse of either polarity, applied as indicated in Fig 12-27. The shape of the impulse shall be 0.3/50 μs (300 ns virtual front time, 50 μs virtual time of half value), as defined in IEC Publication 60 (see Reference [11]).

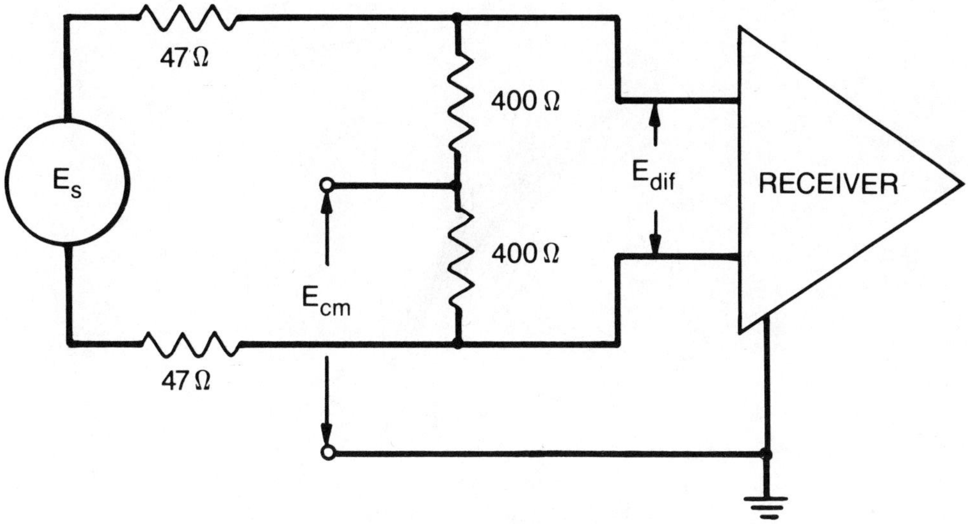

Fig 12-29
Receiver Common-Mode Rejection

NOTE: Tolerance of, and recovery from, the application of the telephony voltages described in 12.10.2 is optional, but the safety requirements of that section are mandatory.

12.6 Medium Dependent Interface (MDI) Specification

12.6.1 Line Interface Connector. 8-pin connectors meeting the requirements of Section 3 and Figs 1 through 5 of ISO/DIS 8877 (see Reference [16]) shall be used as the compatibility interface between the PMA and the medium. The use of other types of connectors, if any, within a PMA or within the medium, although not explicitly prohibited, is outside the scope of this standard.

12.6.2 Connector Contact Assignments. The contacts of the connectors, as depicted in Figs 12-30 and 12-31, shall correspond to signaling circuits as indicated below:

Contact	Signal
1	Upward Data+ (positive for HI signal)
2	Upward Data- (negative for HI signal)
3	Downward Data+ (positive for HI signal)
4	not used by 1BASE5
5	not used by 1BASE5
6	Downward Data- (negative for HI signal)
7	reserved
8	reserved

For DTEs and the upper MDI of hubs, contacts 1 and 2 are used for transmitting and contacts 3 and 6 are used for receiving. For the port MDIs of hubs, however, contacts 1 and 2 are used for receiving and contacts 3 and 6 are used for transmitting.

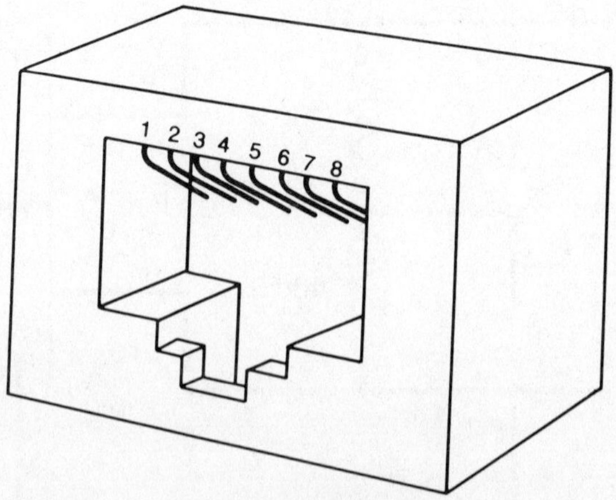

Fig 12-30
DTE and Hub Connector

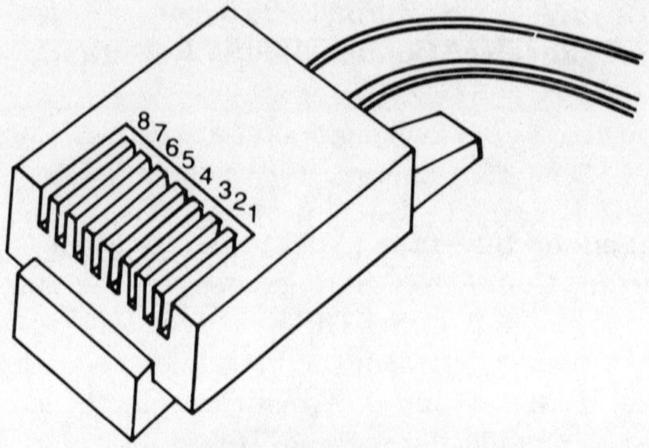

Fig 12-31
Cable Connector

12.6.3 Labeling. To distinguish 1BASE5 connectors from those used for other purposes, it is recommended that appropriate labels be affixed to wall outlets and other connectors. This is particularly important in environments in which the specified 8-contact connectors are used for more than one purpose.

12.7 Cable Medium Characteristics

12.7.1 Overview. A significant number of 1BASE5 networks are expected to utilize in-place building wiring. In this environment, DTEs connect to wall outlets using twisted pair telephone cord. The wall outlets, in turn, connect to wiring closets, where hubs could be located, using standard telephone wiring. This wiring typically consists of 0.4–0.6 mm diameter (26–22 gauge) unshielded twisted pairs.

12.7.2 Transmission Parameters. Each wire pair used to interconnect DTEs and hubs shall meet the requirements of 12.9.3 and also have the following characteristics.

12.7.2.1 Attenuation. Total cable attenuation between a transmitter and the corresponding receiver shall be no more than 6.5 dB at all frequencies between BR/2 and BR, 9.2 dB at frequencies between BR and 2BR, and 13.8 dB at frequencies between 2BR and 4BR.

12.7.2.2 Differential Characteristic Impedance. The magnitude of the differential characteristic impedance at frequency BR, Z_{BR}, of each wire pair used shall be between 80 Ω and 115 Ω. In addition, the magnitude and phase angle of the characteristic impedance at each of the following frequencies shall be within the corresponding ranges indicated:

	Magnitude		Phase Angle	
Frequency	Minimum	Maximum	Minimum	Maximum
BR/4	Z_{BR}	Z_{BR} + 7 Ω	-10°	0°
BR/2	Z_{BR}	Z_{BR} + 5 Ω	-8°	0°
BR	Z_{BR}	Z_{BR}	-6°	0°
2BR	Z_{BR} - 4 Ω	Z_{BR}	-4°	0°
4BR	Z_{BR} - 5 Ω	Z_{BR}	-3°	0°

12.7.2.3 Medium Timing Jitter. Intersymbol interference and reflections due to impedance mismatches between the sections of a cable segment can introduce jitter in the timing of the zero-crossings. A cable segment terminated in 96 Ω shall add no more than ±17 ns, referenced to the transmit clock, of edge jitter when driven with a rectangular signal of magnitude 2.5 V through a source impedance 22 Ω. The driving signal shall be a Manchester-encoded, pseudorandom, sequence of data with a repetition period of at least 511 bits.

NOTE: (1) The reflections caused by splicing two cable sections that have different characteristic impedances (but that each meet the requirements of 12.7.2.2) will not contribute significantly to timing jitter if the splice is within 10 m of either end of the segment.

(2) Branches off a wire pair (often referred to as "bridged taps" or "stubs") will generally cause excessive jitter and so should be avoided.

(3) Jitter can be measured at the receiving end of a segment using an oscilloscope. The oscilloscope is triggered on zero-crossings; the deviation of subsequent zero-crossings from multiples of BT/2 is then observed. The deviation of each zero-crossing must not exceed ±34 ns.

12.7.2.4 Dispersion. Each wire pair shall produce an output signal that meets the zero-crossing edge rate described in 12.5.3.2.1 when driven with a 1 MHz trapezoidal signal of magnitude 2.0 V (that is, 4.0 V peak-to-peak) with edge rate 20 mV/ns.

12.7.3 Coupling Parameters. To avoid excessive coupling of signals between pairs of a cable, the crosstalk and imbalance must be limited.

Crosstalk attenuation is specified with the far end of both the disturbed and the disturbing pairs and the near end of the disturbed pair terminated in 96 Ω.

12.7.3.1 Pair-to-Pair Crosstalk. The near-end, differential, crosstalk attenuation between each wire pair and each other pair in the same cable shall be at least 45 dB at frequencies up to BR and at least $45 - 15 \log_{10}(f/BR)$ dB for each frequency f between BR and 4BR.

12.7.3.2 Multiple-Disturber Crosstalk. The near-end, differential, crosstalk attenuation between multiple disturbing wire pairs and a disturbed pair in the same cable shall be at least 38.5 dB at frequency BR and at least 38.5 - 15 $\log_{10}(f/BR)$ dB for each frequency f between BR and 4BR.

When two or more disturbers are present in a common cable sheath, the multiple-disturber, near-end, crosstalk attenuation (MDNEXT) into each pair, measured in dB, may be determined using the following equations:

$$H_j = \Sigma_{i \neq j} 10^{(-X_{ij}/20)} \cos \theta_{ij}$$

$$V_j = \Sigma_{i \neq j} 10^{(-X_{ij}/20)} \sin \theta_{ij}$$

$$MDNEXT_j = 10 \log_{10}(H_j^2 + V_j^2)$$

where:

i iterates over each disturbing pair
j is the disturbed pair
X_{ij} is the magnitude of the near-end, differential, crosstalk attenuation from pair i to pair j
θ_{ij} is the phase angle of the near-end, differential, crosstalk attenuation from pair i to pair j

If only the probability distribution of X_{ij} is known, then the distribution of MDNEXT can be determined using Monte Carlo methods with that X_{ij} distribution and a phase angle uniformly distributed between 0 and 2π rad.

Note: See Appendix A3 for example computations of MDNEXT distributions.

12.7.3.3 Balance. The longitudinal to metallic balance of the cable, defined as $20 \log_{10}(E_{test}/2E_x)$, where E_{test} is an externally applied voltage, as shown in Fig 12-32, shall exceed 44 dB at all frequencies up to 4BR.

NOTE: The balance of the test equipment (such as the balance of the transformer and the matching of the 300 Ω resistors) must exceed that required of the cable.

12.7.4 Noise Environment. Links used with 1BASE5 shall provide a noise environment no worse than that described below. The total noise environment generally results from two primary contributions: self-crosstalk from other 1BASE5 wire pairs and externally induced impulse noise, typically from telephone ringing and dialing signals, and office machinery. For the purposes of this standard, it can be assumed that the two components contribute independently and so the total error rate can be appropriately split between the two.

12.7.4.1 Impulse Noise. The noise voltage on wire pairs terminated at both ends in 96 Ω, as measured through the following specified filters, shall not exceed the corresponding threshold voltages more than 9 times per 1800 s interval. Following the start of any particular impulse that is counted, any additional impulses shall be ignored (that is, not counted) for a period of 100 μs. Each filter is a 2-pole Butterworth low-pass filter with the indicated cut-off (3 dB point) frequency.

Cut-Off Frequency	Threshold
2 MHz	170 mV
4 MHz	275 mV
10 MHz	560 mV

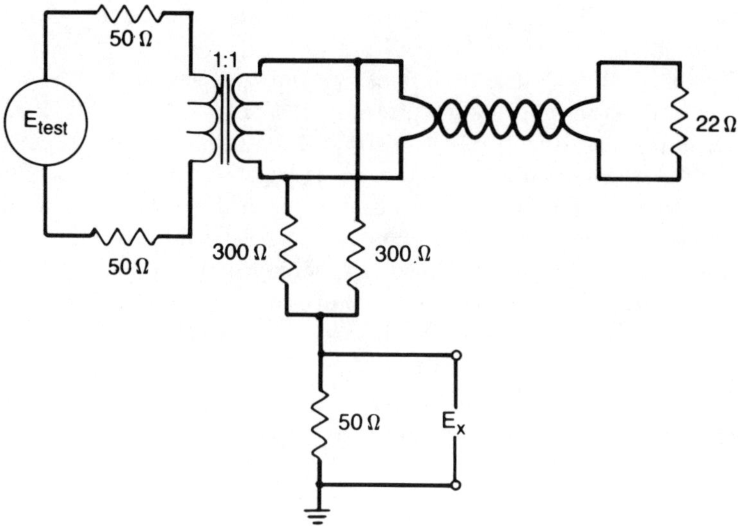

Fig 12-32
Cable Balance Test

The impulse noise occurrence rate changes inversely by one decade for each 7 dB change in the threshold voltage. That is, if the noise occurrence rate is 9 counts per 1800 s at a particular threshold voltage, then a rate of 9 counts per 18 000 s will occur at a threshold 7 dB above that voltage. If a count rate of N counts per 1800 s is measured on a specific cable and filter at the specified voltage threshold, the media noise margin is $7 \log_{10}(9/N)$ dB.

12.7.4.2 Crosstalk. The level of crosstalk noise on a pair depends on the level of the disturbing signal(s) and the crosstalk attenuation from the pair(s) carrying the signal(s). With the maximum transmit level specified in 12.5.3.1, the sinusoidal crosstalk attenuations specified in 12.7.3.1 and 12.7.3.2, and multiple, synchronized, random Manchester disturbers, the peak self-crosstalk (that is, crosstalk from other 1BASE5 signals) noise levels, as measured through the following specified filters, shall be less than or equal to the levels indicated below. Each filter is a 2-pole Butterworth low-pass filter with the indicated cut-off (3 dB point) frequency.

Cut-Off Frequency	Level
2 MHz	105 mV
4 MHz	160 mV

12.8 Special Link Specification

12.8.1 Overview. Some 1BASE5 networks may require extension beyond the limits imposed by 12.7 or, due to the installation environment, may require special media such as optical fiber, high-grade cable, or even free-space transmission. The detailed design of special links that replace standard links for use in such circumstances is beyond the scope of this standard, but the end-to-end characteristics are specified. It shall be the responsibility of the supplier to ensure the proper operation of special links with other 1BASE5 equipment.

12.8.2 Transmission Characteristics. Special links shall meet the overall attenuation, jitter, and dispersion specifications of 12.7.2.1, 12.7.2.3, and 12.7.2.4, respectively. Total noise introduced due to crosstalk or other sources shall not exceed that allowed for standard media, as specified in 12.7.4. To the extent that it affects operability with 1BASE5 transmitters and receivers, special links shall also meet the impedance and balance requirements of 12.7.2.2 and 12.7.3. The delay and preamble loss allowed for special links is specified in 12.9.4.

12.8.3 Permitted Configurations. No more than one special link is permitted in the path between any DTE and the header hub. That is, special links may be installed in parallel but not in series.

NOTE: Special links may be combined with other 1BASE5 components, such as hubs. Such combinations are subject to the performance specifications of this standard only as visible at their external interfaces. For example, explicit MDIs are not required internal to such combinations.

12.9 Timing

12.9.1 Overview. The successful interconnection of multivendor system components mandates that delay and bit loss be allocated fairly and realistically among the various system elements. The balance of this section defines the upper limits of delay and bit loss allocated to each component. These values allow proper operation with the worst-case system configuration of five levels of hubs, special links, maximum-length cable segments throughout the network, and colliding DTEs at extremes of the network.

12.9.2 DTE Timing. DTE Initial Transmit Delay is the time from the first full transition (due to the first OUTPUT_UNIT of preamble) from the MAC to the first full transition (after startup bit loss, if any) at the MDI. This delay shall not exceed 3BT. The startup bit loss shall not exceed 1 bit.

DTEs shall correctly receive frames that are preceded by 13 or more bits of preamble plus 8 bits of <sfd>.

There is a delay between the reception of signal at the PMA input of a DTE and operation of the deferral process in the MAC. Therefore, there is a window in which a DTE may fail to defer to a transmission even after it has arrived at the input. The DTE Deference Delay is the time from the receipt of the first transition of the preamble at the MDI until the last moment that the DTE might start transmitting at the MDI. This delay includes the following components:

(1) The delay from the first input transition at the MDI to CARRIER_ON at the PLS-MAC interface

(2) The delay through the MAC processes from CARRIER_ON to the last moment that a new transmission would miss being deferred

(3) The delay from the first OUTPUT_UNIT at the MAC-PLS interface to the first output transition at the MDI

The DTE Deference Delay shall be no more than 21BT.

The DTE Collision Shutdown Delay is the time from the first CVL or CVH arriving at the MDI of a transmitting DTE until that DTE transmits IDL at that interface. This time shall be no more than 26BT+jamSize=58BT. This limit shall not start until after the <sfd> has been transmitted.

12.9.3 Medium Timing. The Medium Transit Delay is the time from when a signal enters the medium until that signal leaves the medium. This delay shall not exceed 4BT.

12.9.4 Special Link Timing. The Special Link Transit Delay is the time from when a signal enters a special link until that signal leaves the special link. This delay shall not exceed 15BT. The preamble leaving a special link shall be no more than 2 bit cells longer than the preamble sent to that special link and no more than 1 bit cell shorter than the preamble sent to that special link. For the purposes of these limits only, the first bit transmitted shall be considered part of the silence of the preceding IDL unless it meets the requirements for the succeeding bits specified in 12.5.3.1.1 and 12.5.3.1.2.

12.9.5 Hub Timing. Hub Startup Delay is the time from when the first bit cell of the preamble arrives at a hub until the first bit cell (also preamble) leaves that hub. This time shall be no greater than 12BT. The preamble sent by a hub shall be no more than 1 bit cell longer than the preamble sent to that hub or more than 4 bit cells shorter than the preamble sent to that hub. For the purposes of these limits only, the first bit transmitted shall be considered part of the silence of the preceding IDL unless it meets the requirements for the succeeding bits specified in 12.5.3.1.1 and 12.5.3.1.2.

Hub Idle Collision Startup Delay applies to any case in which CP arrives preceded by fewer (or no) bit times of preamble than the Hub Startup Delay. The time from arrival of the first bit cell (either preamble or CP) until the first bit cell leaves the hub shall be no greater than 12BT.

Hub Transit Delay is the time from the arrival of any bit cell at a hub to the transmission of the corresponding bit cell from the hub. This delay shall not exceed 9BT, excluding the cumulative effects of clock tolerance.

The transit (propagation) delay between the upward and downward sides of the Header Hub shall be negligible.

Hub Delay Stretch/Shrink is the increase or decrease in a hub's transit delay due to the effects of differing clock rates. The clock rate tolerance of 0.01% specified in 12.3.2.4.1 and the maximum frame size of 1518 octets specified in 4.4.2.2 yield a maximum stretch or shrink of $(56+8+1518 \cdot 8) \cdot 0.01\% \cdot 2 < 3\text{BT}$, both at any given hub and through an entire network.

Hub Collision Detect Delay is the time required for a hub to detect multiple incoming signals and initiate transmission of CP. The time until transmission of the first CVH or CVL shall be no greater than 21BT.

Hub Active Collision Startup Delay is the time from the arrival of the first CVH or CVL of a CP pattern at a hub that is repeating bit cells until transmission of the first CVH or CVL from the hub. This delay shall be no greater than 12BT in either the upward or downward direction.

Hub Collision Shutdown Delay is the time from IDL arriving at a hub that is passing on or generating CP until that hub starts transmitting IDL. This delay shall be limited to 9BT. The limit is relaxed to 25BT, however, for the upward side of a hub that is generating CP. This extra allowance is made to avoid requiring implementation of a separate <etd> detection mechanism in each port of the hub.

12.10 Safety. Implementors are urged to consult the relevant local, national, and international safety regulations to ensure compliance with the appropriate standards. EIA CB8-1981 (see Annex [12]) provides additional guidance concerning many relevant regulatory requirements.

Sound installation practice, as defined by applicable codes and regulations, shall be followed. ECMA-97 (see Annex [11]) describes safety requirements for local area networks.

12.10.1 Isolation. Each PMA/MDI interface lead shall be isolated from frame ground. This electrical separation shall withstand at least one of the following electrical strength tests:

(1) 1500 V (rms) at 50 to 60 Hz for 60 s, applied as specified in Section 5.3.2 of IEC Publication 950 [13].

(2) 2250 V (dc) for 60 s, applied as specified in Section 5.3.2 of IEC Publication 950 (see Reference [8]).

(3) A sequence of ten 2400 V impulses of alternating polarity, applied at intervals of not less than 1 s. The shape of the impulses shall be 1.2/50 μs (1.2 μs virtual front time, 50 μs virtual time of half value), as defined in IEC Publication 60 (see Reference [11]).

There shall be no insulation breakdown, as defined in Section 5.3.2 of IEC Publication 950 (see Reference [8]), during the test. The resistance after the test shall be at least 2 MΩ, measured at 500 V (dc).

12.10.2 Telephony Voltages. The use of building wiring brings with it the possibility of wiring errors that may connect telephony voltages to 1BASE5 equipment. Other than voice signals (which are very low voltage), the primary voltages that may be encountered are the "battery" and ringing voltages. Although there is no universal standard that constrains them, the following maximums generally apply:

(1) Battery voltage to an on-hook telephone line is about -56 V (dc) applied to the line through a balanced 400 Ω source impedance. This voltage is used to power the telephone instrument and detect the off-hook condition. Source inductance can cause large spikes on disconnect.

(2) Battery voltage to an off-hook telephone line is also about -56 V (dc) applied to the line through a balanced 400 Ω source impedance, but most of the voltage appears across the source impedance because the telephone instrument's impedance is relatively much lower.

(3) Ringing voltage is a composite signal. The first portion can be up to 175 V peak at 20 to 66 Hz, limited by a 100 Ω source resistance or a 400 to 600 Ω source inductive impedance. The second portion is -56 V (dc) limited by a 300 to 600 Ω source impedance. Large spikes can occur at the start and end of each ring.

Although 1BASE5 equipment is not required to survive such wiring hazards without damage, application of any of the above voltages shall not result in any safety hazard.

NOTE: Wiring errors may impose telephony voltages differentially across the 1BASE5 transmitters or receivers. Because the termination resistance likely to be present across a receiver's input is of substantially lower impedance than an off-hook telephone instrument, however, receivers will generally appear to the telephone system as off-hook telephones. Full ring voltages, therefore, will be applied for only short periods of time. Transmitters that are coupled using transformers will similarly appear like off-hook telephones (though perhaps a bit more slowly) due to low resistance of the transformer coil.

ANNEX

ADDITIONAL REFERENCE MATERIAL

The complete Annex to ISO 8802-3 : 1989 [ANSI/IEEE Std 802.3-1988] is included here for convenience and as a means to identify all relevant national standards or related reference material. Some of the references listed herein refer only to the ISO/ANSI/IEEE standard and are not referred to in these Supplements.

NOTE: The following references are a composite of those entries in ANSI/IEEE 802.3-1988, as well as those included in the supplements and is taken from the ISO 8802-3 : 1989 companion document.

(This ANNEX is not a part of ISO 8802-3 : 1989, but is a part of ANSI/IEEE Std 802.3-1988.)

[A1] ANSI/EIA 364A-1987, Standard Test Procedures for Low-Frequency (Below 3 MHz) Electrical Connector Test Procedure.[8]

[A2] ANSI/IEEE Std 770X3.97-1983, IEEE Standard Pascal Computer Programming Language.[9]

[A3] ANSI/IEEE Std 802.3a-1988, Section 10, Type 10BASE2.

[A4] ANSI/IEEE Std 802.3b-1985, Section 11, Type 10BROAD36.

[A5] ANSI/IEEE Std 802.3c-1985, Section 9, Repeater Unit.

[A6] ANSI/IEEE Std 802.3e-1987, Section 12, Type 1BASE5.

[A7] ANSI/NFPA 70-1987, National Electrical Code.[10]

[A8] ANSI/UL 94-1985, Tests for Flammability of Plastic Materials for Parts in Devices and Appliances.[11]

[A9] ANSI/UL 114-1982, Safety Standard for Office Appliances and Business Equipment.

[A10] ANSI/UL 478-1979, Safety Standard for Electronic Data-Processing Units and Systems.

---

[8] All ANSI publications are available from the Sales Department, American National Standards Institute, 1430 Broadway, New York, NY 10018; EIA publications are available from the Standards Sales Department, Electronic Industries Association, 1001 Eye Street, NW, Washington, DC 20006.

[9] IEEE publications are available from the Service Center, Institute of Electrical and Electronics Engineers, 445 Hoes Lane, PO Box 1331, Piscataway, NJ 08855-1331.

[10] NFPA publications are available from Publications Sales, National Fire Protection Association, Batterymarch Park, Quincy, MA 02269.

[11] UL publications are available from Publications Sales, Underwriters Laboratories, Inc, 333 Pfingston Rd, Northbrook, IL 60020.

[A11] ECMA-97 1985), Local Area Networks Safety Requirements.[12]

[A12] EIA CB8-1981, Components Bulletin (Cat 4) List of Approved Agencies, US and Other Countries, Impacting Electronic Components and Equipment.

[A13] FCC Docket 20780-1980 (Part 15), Technical Standards for Computing Equipment. Amendment of Part 15 to redefine an clarify the rules governing restricted radiation devices and low-power communication devices. Reconsidered First Report and Order, April 1980.[13]

[A14] MIL-C-17F-1983, General Specification for Cables, Radio Frequency, Flexible and Semirigid.[14]

[A15] MIL-C-24308B-1983, General Specifications for Connector, Electric, Rectangular, Miniature Polarized Shell, Rack and Panel.

[A16] UL Subject No 758: UL VW-1, Description of Appliance Wiring Material.[15]

[A17] AMP, Inc, Departmental Publication 5525, Design Guide to Coaxial Taps. Harrisburg, PA 17105.

[A18] AMP, Inc, Instruction Sheet 6814, Active Tap Installation. Harrisburg, PA 17105.

[A19] Brinch Hansen, P. The Architecture of Concurrent Programs. Englewood Cliffs, NJ: Prentice Hall, 1977.

[A20] Hammond, J.L., Brown, J.E., and Liu, S.S. Development of a Transmission Error Model and Error Control Model. Technical Report RADC-TR-75-138. Rome: Air Development Center (1975).

[12] ECMA publications are available from European Computer Manufacturers Association, 114 Rue du Rhone, 1204 Geneva, Switzerland.

[13] FCC publications are available from the Federal Communications Commission, Washington, DC 20402.

[14] MIL publications are available from US Navy Publications and Forms Center, 5801 Tabor Avenue, Philadelphia, PA 19120.

[15] Information on this subject is available from Underwriters Laboratories, Inc, 1285 Walt Whitman Road, Melville, NY 11747.

Appendix A
System Guidelines

(This Appendix is not a part of ANSI/IEEE Std 802.3b,c,d, and e, 1989 Edition, Supplements to Carrier Sense Multiple Access with Collision Detection (CSMA/CD), but is included for information only.)

A2. System Parameters and Budgets for 1BASE5

A2.1 Delay Budget. The successful interconnection of multi-vendor system components mandates that the values for bits lost and signal delays be allocated fairly and realistically among the various system elements. The following table summarizes and indicates the derivation of some of the delays specified in 12.9. The breakdowns shown for the parameters are illustrative only; implementors are free to make other allocations of delay *within* a device so long as the specifications of 12.9 are not violated.

Component	Delay (BT)
DTE Initial Transmit Delay (see 12.9.2)	**3**
DTE Deference Delay (see 12.9.2)	**21**
unsquelch	3
Carrier detect	5
MAC detects carrier and defers	10
DTE Initial Transmit Delay	3
DTE Collision Shutdown Delay (see 12.9.2)	**58**
detect CP and report SIGNAL_ERROR	10
detect SIGNAL_ERROR and start jamming	16
jamSize	32
Medium Transit Delay (see 12.9.3)	**4**
Special Link Transit Delay (see 12.9.4)	**15**
Hub Startup Delay (see 12.9.5)	**12**
unsquelch	4
half fill FIFO	6
analogue of DTE Initial Transmit Delay	3
Hub Idle Collision Startup Delay (see 12.9.5) (same as Hub Startup Delay)	**12**
Hub Transit Delay (see 12.9.5)	**9**
half fill FIFO	6
analogue of DTE Initial Transmit Delay	3
Hub Delay Stretch/Shrink (see 12.9.5) ((preamble + <sfd> + maxFrameSize) · 0.01% · 2)	**3**
Hub Collision Detect Delay (see 12.9.5)	**21**
unsquelch	3
detect collision	6

Hub Transit Delay	9
First CVL or CVH may be preceded by CD0s and CD1s	3
Hub Active Collision Startup Delay (see 12.9.5)	**12**
Hub Transit Delay	9
First CVL or CVH may be preceded by CD0s and CD1s	3
Hub Collision Shutdown Delay (downward) (see 12.9.5) (same as Hub Transit Delay)	**9**
Hub Collision Shutdown Delay (upward) (see 12.9.5)	**25**
detect loss of carrier	20
clear FIFO, if necessary	2
analogue of DTE Initial Transmit Delay	3

A2.2 Minimum Frame Length Determination. The minimum frame length for 1BASE5 is determined using the values specified in 4.4.2.2 and 12.9, applied to the following (worst) case:

(1) DTE 1, connected to Hub 1 at a network extremity, transmits a message upward toward Hub 5.

(2) There is a special link in the path between Hub 1 and Hub 5.

(3) DTE 2, also connected to Hub 1, transmits, just missing deferring to the downward signal from DTE 1 that was wrapped around at Hub 5.

(4) DTE 3, also connected to Hub 1, receives the transmission from DTE 1.

(5) Hub 1 generates CP which travels up and then back down the network to inform DTE 1 and DTE 2 that a collision has occurred on their messages.

(6) DTE 1 and DTE 2 continue to transmit until they have received CP, reacted to it, and completed their jams.

(7) DTE 3 continues to receive until the end of CP.

The minimum frame length must allow both of the following conditions to be met:

(1) DTE 1 is still sending when CP is received and recognized.

(2) DTE 3 can discard the message fragment it receives because it is too short.

Event	Bits	Total
DTE 1 → DTE 2		
DTE Initial Transmit Delay	3	3
8 · Medium Transit Delay	32	35
2 · Special Link Transit Delay	30	65
10 · Hub Startup Delay	120	185
DTE Deference Delay	21	206
DTE 2 → HUB 1 CP		
Medium Transit Delay	4	210
Hub Collision Detect Delay	21	231
HUB 1 CP → HUB 5 CP		
3 · Medium Transit Delay	12	243
Special Link Transit Delay	15	358

4 · max(Hub Startup Delay, Hub Active Collision Startup Delay, Hub Idle Collision Startup Delay)	48	306
HUB 5 CP → DTE 1 receives CP		
5 · Hub Active Collision Startup Delay	60	366
4 · Medium Transit Delay	16	382
Special Link Transit Delay	15	397
DTE 1 receives CP → DTE 1 stops transmitting		
DTE Collision Shutdown Delay	58	455
COMPUTATION OF MINIMUM FRAME SIZE		
original preamble + <sfd>	-64	391 = data bits transmitted
5 · (Hub Collision Shutdown Delay (upward) -Hub Transit Delay)	80	471
5 · (Hub Collision Shutdown Delay (downward) -Hub Transit Delay)	0	471
tiny fraction of Hub Delay Stretch/Shrink	0	471 = data bits received

The minimum frame length must exceed both the maximum number of bits sent before recognizing CP (391 - jamSize = 359) and the maximum collision fragment size (471), as computed above. The 1BASE5 system value for minimum frame length has been set at 512 bits, which exceeds both of these values with a margin for error.

A2.3 Jitter Budget. The total edge jitter of the signals on each link must be limited to allow proper decoding at the receiver. The following budget has been used to allocate jitter to the indicated components that contribute to the total jitter on each link:

Component	Jitter
Transmitter skew	±10 ns
Cable intersymbol interference	9
Cable reflections	8
Reflections due to receiver termination mismatch	5
Total	±32 ns

The cable intersymbol interference and reflection allowances form the basis for the limit specified in 12.7.2.3; the reflection component is sufficient to allow a single 20 Ω impedance mismatch anywhere along a cable segment. The receiver-mismatch allowance is derived from the reflection attenuation specified in 12.5.3.2.4. The total forms the basis for the specification in 12.5.3.2.2.

The remainder of the jitter that can be tolerated by the Manchester decoder in a receiver is reserved to allow for distortion of the signal due to noise, receiver threshold offset, receiver skew, and receiver sampling timing error.

A simple clocked receiver/decoder with an 8 MHz sampling rate (the worst case allowed for in the design of this standard), can achieve proper decoding with up to ±125 ns of jitter between two edges, which is equivalent to ±62.5 ns on each edge. Other receiver designs may tolerate more edge jitter. For example, a 6 MHz sampling rate would allow up to ±83.33 ns of jitter on each edge and a 16 MHz sampling rate allows up to ±93.75 ns of jitter.

It may be necessary to use a low-pass filter as part of the receiver to reduce the noise level seen by that receiver (see 12.7.4 for a description of the noise environment). A filter that reduces the noise may also have an effect on the amplitude and edge rate of the received signal. The filtered signal's edge rate near the zero-crossing is used in the critical translation from mV of noise and receiver offset into ns of jitter.

An example receiver design using an 8 MHz sampling rate and a 2 MHz Butterworth input filter might be based on the following jitter budget:

Component	Jitter
Input jitter (from above)	±32 ns
Noise and receiver threshold offset	19.5
Receiver skew (analog)	4
Receiver skew (digital)	7
Total	±62.5 ns

Fig A4
MDNEXT Cumulative Probability Distribution

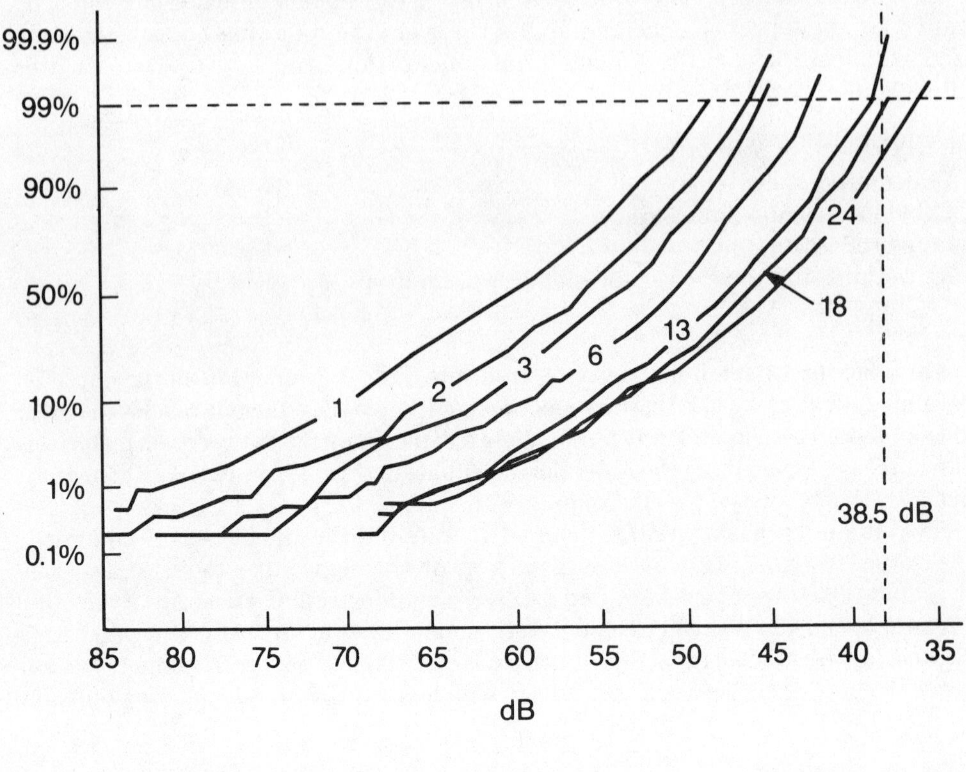

The two primary contributors to noise in a 1BASE5 cable are self-crosstalk and impulse noise (see 12.7.4). Because it is unlikely that both will be present at their 1% worst-case levels on any particular cable, the required bit error rate attributable to each source can be set at half of the one in 10^8 error rate required by 12.5.3.2.6.

Crosstalk noise is specified to be no more than 105 mV (peak) through a 2 MHz filter (see 12.7.4.2). Because crosstalk is present for the entire transmission of a packet, some crosstalk will coincide with the most sensitive part of the received signal. Therefore, the receiver must operate without error in the presence of this 105 mV of noise.

Impulse noise has a peak amplitude of 170 mV for $\leq$0.005 counts/s through the 2 MHz filter (see 12.7.4.1). This threshold does not directly correlate to jitter, however, because the derivation of the 62.5 ns jitter tolerance for an 8MHz clock assumed worst-case sampling error. Assuming a random phasing of the sampling clock to the received signals, it can be shown that the 170 mV of noise is equivalent to a level of 85 mV with a worst-phase clock.

Jitter due to noise should be computed using the larger of the above two levels. The 105 mV for crosstalk noise, therefore, should be added to 50 mV for receiver threshold offset and the result should be divided by the edge rate of the filtered signal near the zero-crossing (7.9 mV/ns for the 2 MHz filter), yielding the 19.5 ns indicated above.

A3. Example Crosstalk Computation for Multiple Disturbers

A method for computing multiple-disturber, near-end, crosstalk attenuation (MDNEXT) into each 1BASE5 pair is specified in 12.7.3.2. This appendix provides example computations of MDNEXT using that method when only the distribution of X_{ij} is known.

The single-disturber probability distribution curve (labelled "1") shown in Fig A4 is based on actual measurement of 25-pair, 24-gauge, unshielded, twisted pair cable. The remaining probability distribution curves (labelled with the number of disturbing pairs) were computed using Monte Carlo simulation. To compute each sample $MDNEXT_j$ for N disturbers, N values of crosstalk attenuation (X_i) were chosen from the single-disturber distribution and N values of crosstalk phase (θ_i) were chosen from a uniform distribution between 0 and 2π rad. These values were then used with the following equations to compute $MDNEXT_j$:

$$H_j = \Sigma_{1\leq i\leq N}\, 10^{(-X_i/20)} \cos \theta_i$$

$$V_j = \Sigma_{1\leq i\leq N}\, 10^{(-X_i/20)} \sin \theta_i$$

$$MDNEXT_j = 10 \log_{10}(H_j^2 + V_j^2)$$

Iterating this process several hundred times, each time producing a single $MDNEXT_j$ sample, resulted in distributions for MDNEXT that are summarized in the following table and Fig A4:

Disturbers	Iterations	MDNEXT: Mean	Std. Dev.	99%
1		61.2 dB	7.0 dB	48.6 dB
2	500	57.2	6.2	46.4
3	500	55.1	5.8	45.2
6	500	52.0	5.7	42.5
13	1000	48.5	5.4	39.1
18	500	47.1	5.3	37.8
24	500	45.9	5.9	36.2

Because two pairs are used for each 1BASE5 connection, the entries in this table for 18 and 24 disturbers are not applicable for normal installation of 25-pair cables. Furthermore, telephone cables with larger numbers of pairs are often constructed using sub-bundles of 25 pairs each and so might yield similar results (for example, the curves for 13 or fewer disturbers would be the most applicable ones).